Caning: Educational Rite and Tradition

By

JOSEPH A. MERCURIO

Syracuse University Division
of Special Education and
Rehabilitation and the
Center on Human Policy

FOURTH IN A SERIES:
SEGREGATED SETTINGS AND
THE PROBLEM OF CHANGE

BURTON BLATT
SEYMOUR B. SARASON
HARRIETT D. BLANK
EDITORS

LB
3013
M4

Additional copies of this book may be ordered from:
SYRACUSE UNIVERSITY PRESS
Box 8, University Station
Syracuse, New York 13210

Manufactured in the United States of America

THE CENTER ON HUMAN POLICY
is currently supported by
GRANTS NO. 56-P-71003-2-01 AND
55-P-10158-2-01 from the
Department of Health, Education and Welfare,
Social and Rehabilitation Service

To
Carolyn

Acknowledgments

This study was conducted under the auspices of a Fulbright-Hays Fellowship to New Zealand. The data were gathered during the period March, 1969, to January, 1970.

I wish to thank the many people who were instrumental to the success and completion of the project.

Richard Dawson, former Secretary of the Society For the Abolition of Corporal Punishment in New Zealand Schools, sent me materials and advice from New Zealand during the exploratory phases of the research.

John Watson, Director of the New Zealand Council for Educational Research, offered advice and encouragement regarding the feasibility of the project and gave willingly of his time and cooperation whenever I visited him in Wellington.

Professor Philip Lawrence, Chairman of the Department of Education of the University of Canterbury, served as my Fulbright sponsor and research advisor. He welcomed my wife and me to New Zealand and saw that our immediate needs were taken care of. He gave freely of his time, counsel, and criticism from beginning to end. I am grateful to him for his help and for the critical discussions we had in the testing and revision of our ideas.

I shall be forever indebted to Mr. Charles F. Caldwell, Headmaster of Christchurch Boys' High School, for accepting me into his school, and for his readiness to be of every possible assistance throughout the course of the research. His willingness to have me around for a year is deeply appreciated. I hope that his faith in my ability to see clearly and to report honestly has been justified.

As in all research of this kind, responsibilities exist regarding the confidentiality and anonymity of the people involved. With the exception of the Headmaster, the school's historical personalities, and the identity of the school itself, the names mentioned in the study are fictitious. I want to thank the Board of Governors of Christchurch Boys' High School for permission to use the name of the school in the interests of bringing the study to life. I hope that their faith in my ability to interpret clearly and fairly also is justified.

I am grateful to the boys of the school, their teachers, and their parents for accepting me and helping me to find out what I wanted to know.

They were unfailingly cooperative while allowing themselves to be the subjects of an outsider's investigation.

Heather and Bridget—the two friendly secretaries of the University of Canterbury History Department—typed the 600 pages of field notes and memoranda produced during the field work phase of the project.

I owe a special thanks to my thesis advisors, Dr. Thomas F. Green, and Dr. William Pooler of Syracuse University, and Dr. William R. Burch of Yale University. As I tried to turn a large, rough assortment of field notes into final form, they gave freely and regularly of their advice and criticisms. My gratitude to them is unbounded.

Finally, I wish to thank my wife Carolyn for her invaluable observations, suggestions, and reactions to my findings during the course of the study, and not least, for having borne well the emotional burdens that involvement in a project such as this entails.

Introduction

Horace Mann probably put it as well as anyone in his reference to corporal punishment in the schools more than 100 years ago:

> Possibly on no other subject pertaining to education is there so marked a diversity or rather hostility of opinion as on this; nor on any other, such perseverance, not to say, obstinacy, in adhering to opinions formed.*

Things have not changed much since then. Corporal punishment in the schools is as lively, significant, and possibly even more contentious an issue now than ever before, while individual opinion regarding its employment appears to be no less divided and no less obstinate.

•Teachers in Dallas, Texas, for instance, rebelled not long ago when the superintendent ordered strict observance of an official policy that limited the right to paddle to principals. Carrying their fight to the public, the teachers argued that growing student dissent, drug abuse, and defiance made paddling necessary. They eventually won reversal of the superintendent's order. In Pittsburgh, 73 percent of the teachers recently signed a petition demanding that a ban against spanking—won two years earlier by an anti-corporal punishment group—be lifted. And in Cleveland, Ohio, after a mother filed suit contending that her son was paddled against her instructions, teachers geared up to fight for authority to paddle students. Opponents of corporal punishment in the schools —including civil liberties groups and some parents—are dismayed and angered by the reappearance of spanking and the paddle. Many agree with Dr. Benjamin Spock, who argues that paddling "increases the defiance, not the cooperation" of maladjusted children. But in a typically worded rebuttal to anti-corporal punishment forces, Albert Fondy, president of the Pittsburgh Teachers Federation, stated, "Until somebody comes up with an alternative, we'll support it."

Heated disputes over corporal punishment in the schools by no means are confined to the United States. A somewhat smug-sounding passage from the December 6, 1971, issue of *Newsweek* magazine (U.S. edition) entitled, "Spare the Rod?" illustrates the point:

* Horace Mann, *Lectures on Education,* Lecture 7, "On School Punishment," delivered in 1840, first published in 1845 (Boston: Ide and Dutton), p. 306.

British educators, with their increasing emphasis on "open classrooms," have won much praise for progressive thinking in recent years. But an educational reform decreed in London last week served to demonstrate that many a British schoolmaster still looks on "Tom Brown's School Days" as the last serious educational text. When the Inner London Education Authority announced that the ancient practice of caning will be abolished in the city's primary schools, traditionbound teachers all over Britain angrily responded that the best way to hold a young scholar's attention is to beat his backside once in a while. "We oppose abolition of the cane," declared Edward Chandler, head of the London Schoolmasters' Association. "It must be kept as the ultimate deterrent." The new prohibition on corporal punishment, however, will not take effect until Jan. 1, 1973, which ought to permit the pro-caning forces to get in a few last licks.

Nor is the issue a dead one in New Zealand, the country in which this study was conducted. There one finds, on the one hand, groups such as The Society for the Abolition of Corporal Punishment in New Zealand Schools, and the Anti-Corporal Punishment Coordinating Committee pushing hard for the repeal of the practice, and on the other, a non-organized, yet highly influential collection of parents, teachers, administrators, and surprisingly, more than a few pupils, pressing with equal vigor for its retention. Nothing better illustrates the growing contention over the issue of corporal punishment in New Zealand schools—to say nothing of the all too human propensity for jumping to conclusions—than an inquiry I received in October, 1971, from a feature writer of a leading New Zealand newspaper:

Dear Dr. Mercurio:
In the midst of yet another controversy on corporal punishment in New Zealand schools, sparked by the president of the post-Primary Teachers' Association saying he'd like it to go, a Christchurch Boys' High School teacher writing to the Christchurch Star asserts that an American educationist soon will publish a thesis in which he depicts child-beating in New Zealand schools as a huge success.
Inquiries elicit the information that you are the American who is about to publish.
If this is so and if, in fact, you see some good in New Zealand schools' "authoritarian" discipline, could you please let us have either relevant quotes or photo-copies of the relevant pages from the thesis.

And yet, for all the arguments, or for that matter, all the research on this subject, no one has ever taken a lengthy, detailed look at corporal punishment as practiced under the conditions of school life—that is to say, no one has yet gone into a specific setting in the role of disinterested participant-observer and studied corporal punishment over an extended period as an ongoing, "working," institutionalized practice. Consequently, scant attention has been paid to an entire series of questions such as: What does the practice of corporal punishment in the schools look like from the point of view of the participants? How do pupils and teachers not only view, but react to its administration in live situations? In other words, what is the meaning of corporal punishment to those involved with its practice? And how and under what conditions does such meaning develop? What is the relationship of the practice to the values, demands, and expectations of the larger school community? Does the practice itself serve purposes of an extradisciplinary nature? If so, what are these purposes? And again, what is their relationship to the school's —and ultimately the larger community's—demands and expectations of its members? These, of course, are the kinds of questions with which this study is concerned, and which, in my estimation, are crucial to the understanding and assessment of both the phenomenon and the institution of corporal punishment in the schools.

In closing, I ought to say something about why I had to go all the way to New Zealand to study corporal punishment in the schools, since obviously there is no lack of material on this subject in the United States. My reasons, though possibly academically "suspect," are humanly quite understandable. Four successive years of graduate study left me much in need of a change of scene, especially if I was to muster the necessary energy and motivation to "do a dissertation." New Zealand was well off the beaten path. It presented no language barrier. And I had not been there before. It looked to be a most scenic country, replete with long sandy beaches for swimming, magnificent alpine mountains for tramping and climbing, and ample snowfields for almost year-round skiing. The primary consideration of where to go having been resolved, the remaining one of what to study when I got there somehow took care of itself.

J.M.

Table of Contents

Tables

that social groups develop systems of symbols which are shared collectively by the groups' members, and around which the groups' activities are organized. As the participants in these groups interact with one another, they take one another's perspectives toward their own actions. They assume one another's roles. In so doing, they interpret and assess their activity in communal terms.

> The complex cooperative processes and activities and institutional functionings of human society are also possible only insofar as every individual involved in them or belonging to that society can take the general attitudes of all other such individuals with reference to these processes and activities and institutional functions and to the organized social whole of experiential relations and interactions thereby constituted and can direct his own behavior accordingly. . . . And only through the taking by individuals of the attitude or attitudes of the generalized other toward themselves is the existence of a universe of disclosure, as that system of common or social meanings which thinking presupposes as its context, rendered possible.[1]

Group membership, on this view, is a symbolic rather than a physical affair. The symbols that arise during the life of the group are internalized by its members so as to comprise the meanings which are shared and held in common by them. Herein lies the significance of "symbolic" in the phrase symbolic interaction. Individuals' actions acquire symbolic significance as they attain the character of being meaningful to the members of the group. Insofar as the meanings of actions are in this manner shared, there arises the possibility of collective action. Individual action then takes place as the individual attempts to conduct himself in a manner consistent with the attitudes, demands, and expectations of others in the group. The nature of the collective action of which he is a participant thus serves both as explanation and justification for what he does.

Mead further notes that the manner in which things obtain meaning for people is not the result of a simple two-way exchange between an individual and some object/stimulus or event. Rather the process is a much more complex triadic one:

> . . . objects are constituted in terms of meanings within the social process of experience and behavior through the mutual adjustment to one another of the responses or actions of the various individual organisms involved in that process . . . the logical structure of meaning is to be found in the threefold relationship of gesture to adjustive response and to the resultant of the given social act. Response on the part of the second

[1] George Herbert Mead, *Mind, Self, and Society,* edited by Charles W. Morris (Chicago: University of Chicago Press, 1934), pp. 155–56.

organism to the gesture of the first is the interpretation and brings out the meaning of that gesture . . . the basis of meaning is thus objectively there in social conduct or in nature in its relation to such conduct. Meaning is a content of an object which is dependent upon the relation of an organism or group of organisms to it.[2]

The concept of *perspective* is used in this study to analyze the ideas and actions which constitute for participants the meaning of corporal punishment, and is defined as follows:

> . . . a coordinated set of ideas and actions a person uses in dealing with some problematic situation . . . a person's ordinary way of thinking and feeling about and acting in such a situation. These thoughts and actions are coordinated in the sense that the actions flow reasonably, from the actor's perspective, from the ideas contained in the perspective. Similarly, the ideas can be seen by an observer to be one of the possible sets of ideas which might form the underlying rationale for the person's actions and are seen by the actor as providing a justification for acting as he does.[3]

The formula for analysis in this study then is that, under certain conditions, largely socially created, certain phenomena come to hold certain meanings for central individuals or groups of individuals. These meanings are social in nature insofar as they inhere not in the phenomenon itself, but rather in participants' mutually adjustive responses to one's attitudes and expectations. The meanings of things can thus be stated in terms of the ideas and actions used by people in handling problematic situations, in other words, as an expression of their perspectives on things.

The area of interest of the study can now be translated into the following problem: What are the perspectives which pupils, teachers, and parents create to deal with corporal punishment under the conditions of school life? The study which follows is concerned with more than the mere documentation of participant perspectives on corporal punishment, of course. Additionally, it is an attempt to answer questions suggested by that problem, such as: How do those involved with the practice of corporal punishment not only view, but react to its implementation in live situations? How and to what extent do the words of the participant correspond to their actions? What is the meaning of corporal punishment to the participants? How and under what condi-

[2] *Ibid.*, pp. 77, 80.
[3] Howard S. Becker, Blanche Geer, Everett C. Hughes, and Anselm L. Strauss, *Boys in White: Student Culture in Medical School* (Chicago: University of Chicago Press, 1961), p. 34.

tions does it emerge? How and why does the meaning of corporal punishment differ among teachers, pupils, and parents? Does the practice serve purposes beyond those which the participants think it serves? If so, what are these purposes? And what is their relation to the school's— and ultimately the larger community's—demands and expectations of its members?

Research Methods

I used the method of participant observation to study corporal punishment under the conditions of school life. The method, as well as a more complete description of my research activities, appear in the methodological appendix. Briefly, participant observation is a technique in which an observer participates in the everyday life of the people whom he wishes to learn something about. The participant-observer looks at what is happening around him, listens to what is said, queries people over some length of time about the significance of their actions and motives, and tries to explain what is going on. He usually takes lots of notes, mostly in private. He is highly receptive to the possibility of new, previously untested hypothses. Throughout, he endeavors to document and understand the meaning of some social phenomenon to those who have participated before, during, and after its occurrence.

As "observer-in-residence" at Christchurch Boys' High School, I went to classes, followed the people I studied through their daily rounds —watching what they did, when, with whom and under what circumstances—questioned hundreds of people formally and informally in a variety of situations both in and out of school, attended gatherings of all kinds of school organizations and activities, and participated in numerous other aspects of school life. As a guest of the school, however, I did not assume any of its formal obligations. I was not a teacher, nor did I pretend to be a pupil, though I made it my business to know both these groups well. My role, with good reason, was an impartial one. Since I was interested in the perspectives of pupils and staff alike (not to mention parents), I could not afford to be seen by either group as taking sides with respect to possible differences of opinion between them. To have taught classes in the interests of more fully experiencing the faculty's point of view, for example, would have placed me in the position of disciplinarian; this invariably would have compromised my role of confidant *vis-à-vis* boys. To have been overly "chummy" with the latter, by the same token, could have hampered my relations with the faculty. In either case, the study's objectives stood to suffer.

There was another reason for adopting an impartial, at times even "quiet" role. The faculty at Boys' High had a suspicion of "educators." [4] Had I been regarded by them as an agitator or a threat I would have been asked to leave the school immediately. That I had gauged the situation correctly and assumed an appropriate stance was confirmed during a conversation with the school's Headmaster months later:

> "I would like to know in all honesty why you ever let me—a virtual outsider—into your school in the first place," I asked. "Quite honestly," he explained, "I let you in as an experiment. I liked your look. But it's like a business transaction, you know. First you ask yourself what you can get out of this for the school. Second, you ask what this person can get out of it for himself. Frankly, the first week I waited . . . for any staff to come into my office and say, 'Who's this bloke Mercurio anyway?' . . . then you'd simply have been invited to leave the school that first week. But you handled it so completely right . . . it's been a pleasure having you."
>
> OCTOBER 1969

With the exception of the Headmaster, no one at the school was told of my specific interest in corporal punishment. The decision to keep secret this aspect of the study was not an easy one. No one genuinely enjoys spying on people while simultaneously trying to maintain honest and sincere relationships with them. On the other hand—mostly due to the potential sensitivity of my topic—I did not feel I could discuss all my purposes directly with the subjects. To have been regarded as "that Yank bloke poking his nose into the way we cane boys" conceivably could have resulted in the defeat of one of the study's major objectives, namely, to catch participants' everyday patterns of action much as they would occur in the absence of outside intrusion. Furthermore, the nature of the study required that I treat my topic as an interrelated part of a larger picture. To study participant perspectives on corporal punishment is to relate that point of view to the functioning of the school as a whole. Moreover, I did not want to be seen by the participants as concentrating on one aspect of the school's operation to the exclusion of all else. First, this might have narrowed their responses to my ques-

[4] Austin Mitchell notes of the "plight" of the intelligentsia in New Zealand that, "intellectuals are thin on ground, their views largely discounted because they are not 'practical' men . . . pressure against the dissenter still remains: the man with a vision, such as Dr. Sutch, can become a danger. The man who refuses to knuckle under, such as Gordon Bick, is exposed to a New Zealand clobbering machine which is quickly trundled into operation for instant character assassination." Austin Mitchell, *Politics and People In New Zealand* (Christchurch, New Zealand: Whitcombe and Tombs Ltd., 1969), p. 313.

tions. Second, it most probably would have limited my working knowledge of the school. Thus, only the Headmaster was informed of my real purpose. The rest of the school's members were told that I was there to look at the policies and practices of the school from their point of view—something that had never before been attempted at this school, nor, to the best of my knowledge, any other school in New Zealand. It was a statement of purpose that I felt was both honest and inoffensive. As a definition of my intentions, it was understandable and of interest to the school's constituents, yet was compatible with my own aims and objectives.

On the final day of the academic year I informed the staff of the highlights and major findings of the study, including the reasons for keeping secret my specific interest in corporal punishment. Their response was understanding and good-natured. "Well done," "Completely objective," and "You sure pulled one over on us," were typical of their reactions. The good-humored comment of an older, slightly arthritic master as I passed through the school's doors for the last time is worth noting:

> I hope you will note somewhere in your thesis, Joe, that there are some of us who are no longer physically capable of caning.
>
> DECEMBER 1969

Handling the Data

Participant observation typically produces a large body of qualitatively rich but unsystematized material. The nearly 600 pages of typewritten field notes accumulated over the course of the study proved no exception to this tendency. The analysis of such material can be handled in many ways. In this study, the analysis is comparatively straightforward. I have combed my notes for all the material bearing on the problem under consideration, and have developed a series of statements and generalizations on the subject of corporal punishment as it is practiced at Christchurch Boys' High School.

Except for noting the relative frequency of the responses of the participants to certain kinds of events, the study's findings are not significantly supported by statistics. This is because the data of participant observation are qualitative in character. They do not readily lend themselves to standard statistical research techniques.

A final word is in order concerning the use of quotations and excerpts from the field notes. These appear frequently and at length throughout

7

the study, and are presented with several purposes in mind. First, they offer a "feel" for the specific character of participants' concerns. Second, they serve as a basis for considering alternative formulations to those presented in the analysis; this is especially evident with the lengthier quotes. And finally, they are examples of the kind of evidence which stands in support of the study's findings and conclusions.

Chapter 2

Christchurch Boys' High School

I didn't know if I was going to like working here. My husband is an old boy,[1] you see. When we were young and courting we ran around with

This study looks at the perspectives that participants develop toward corporal punishment in a particular place—Christchurch Boys' High School. Before proceeding to the analysis of that problem, it is important that the reader have some appreciation of: (1) the social and physical environment in relation to which these perspectives develop, (2) the relationship between the constraints of the system and the ideas and actions of the participants, and (3) the character of the participants' interpersonal relationships.

A Traditional Setting for a Traditional School

Boys' High School is situated in scenic Christchurch, allegedly one of the most English of cities outside England. A census count of slightly more than 250,000 makes it the largest population center of the South Island of New Zealand.

Looking like something out of Tom Brown's School Days, Boys' High sits two miles west of the city's main center, on the edge of the district of Fendalton, one of the acknowledged "better" of Christchurch's several residential areas. A traditional looking, immaculately kept two-story red brick structure partly covered with ivy houses most of the classrooms. The rest of the grounds consist of an arts and crafts building, a

---

[1] "Old boy" is an English term for an alumnus of a school.
his friends, also old boys . . . it was always school, school, school. That's all they ever talked about. I thought, this school can't be that special. But the minute I came through the doors . . . I can't explain it . . . it's just something you feel . . . the tradition . . . this school . . . is most like what I think an English school should be like. . . . I suppose other schools will have this tradition some day. No, I guess they'll never have it. It's this old building. The new schools are all so modern.
OFFICE STAFF MEMBER, SEPTEMBER 1969

woodwork shop, a pottery shack, a drama hut, a camera club room, a bicycle shed, and several smaller classrooms. For the sports-minded—which includes practically everyone, since participation in sports is compulsory—there is an outdoor swimming pool, a tennis court, a shooting range, an inside basketball court, and of course, a large, well-groomed playing field to accommodate the vast turnouts for Rugby, cricket, soccer, and field hockey. A nearby youth hostel, owned and operated by the school, offers room, board, and adult supervision to approximately 75 boys coming from homes outside the main area. To the rear of the school, the Avon River meanders lazily past spreading eucalyptus and weeping willow trees. To the front is a commanding view of the frontal range of the Southern Alps. The entire campus exudes a kind of "Old World" charm.

The impression maintains itself as one enters the main building through two huge wooden doors at the front. The furniture on the inside is old-looking, but sturdy and usable. Many of the boys sit at desks once occupied by their fathers. Carving one's initials on tabletops appears to be—and to have been—a favorite diversion from more serious matters.

Tradition is both a spiritual and a physical attribute of the school. A total of 557 photographs, plaques, and assorted memorabilia adorn the walls and corridors from one end of the building to the other. They stand as a tribute to the school's sporting record, its successful old boys, its former masters, its celebrations, its war dead, its past. They are a constant reminder to all concerned of what it means to be an integral part of an honored, long-standing, and above all, traditional establishment.

The School and the Community

Boys' High is a state-sponsored, state-financed institution. A Board of Governors is the highest governing body of the school. It consists of a chairman, deputy chairman, secretary, two representatives each of the University of Canterbury and the old boys, four representatives of the parents, and one representative of the Canterbury Education Board.

The school is subject to periodic evaluation by an inspector from the New Zealand Department of Education. Its relationship to the latter otherwise is one of basic independence. Barring gross breaches of indiscretion, it is free to run its own show. Its Headmaster—the one man perhaps most responsible for running the show—is answerable chiefly to the school's Board of Governors:

> "Just how free are you in running this school?" I asked him. "How much, if at all, do you feel the weight of outside pressures—parents,

Board of Governors, the community, and so forth?" He leaned back in his chair and paused to consider the question, then replied, "I run this school as I want to. Completely. But I know that if I take one step in the wrong direction, I'll have ten members of the Board of Governors who will come along and tell me so—politely, mind you—but they'll tell me."

HEADMASTER, OCTOBER 1969

Still, for all that is left to its discretion in the sphere of administration, the school does not, would not, indeed could not operate without regard for the larger social setting of which it is only a part. It is accountable in varying degrees to other groups, organizations, and institutions in the area who give things to it, and who require things of it. Training colleges supply it with teachers, parents supply it with pupils, the state provides it with financial support, friends and old boys provide it with moral support, a Board of Governors oversees its operation, and the business and university communities receive and pass judgment on its product. Viewed realistically, the school and the community operate in relation to one another on a businesslike basis. The community is in the position of supplying the raw materials; the school is charged with the responsibility for coming up with an acceptable finished result.

Yet whereas the larger community has the capacity to limit what the school can do, just as it can create opportunities for what can be done, the school exerts a considerably less powerful counterhold on the larger community. Admittedly, the school plays a crucial role in the educative process whereby some make it better in life than others; certainly it decides, up to a point, who goes on to the university and who does not; it even dictates, within accepted limits, which pupils it will take and which it will not, sending a shiver or two up the spines of more than one set of waiting parents in the process. Yet, for all this, the school is a contributing, not a controlling agency, a conservative rather than innovative organization. It tends to reflect the social pattern instead of setting the pace. It conforms to society's norms and expectations rather than holding them up to question. Ruler supreme within the confines of its own fiefdom, Boys' High—not unlike most of society's agencies of learning everywhere—is the handmaiden of a larger kingdom.

The school, with an acute awareness of what ultimately is expected of it, works toward certain ends. This is not to suggest that it has in mind a "goal" as such. Rather, the goal (or goals) of the school are best understood as a combination of the ends, collective and individual, of each of its constituents. Indeed, because the ends in view of its members are at the same time multiple and diverse, the goals of the school

11

are not always in agreement. Occasionally, they even may operate at cross-purposes.

Whatever the ends of the school's participants, however, they must be arrived at realistically, that is, as a result of having taken into account the demands, expectations, and possibilities for action inherent in the environmental context. In this way, the school comes to terms with a world beyond its ivy-draped walls. It creates a system of symbols, ideas, and attendant patterns of behavior which enable it to cope with a community larger than its own, and with the restrictions which this larger community places on its actions.

One reason for being concerned with the school's adaptation to its environment is that the nature of that adaptation usually is transferred—through the actions of the school's teachers and administrative personnel, and through pupils' parents—into a series of demands and constraints on the pupils themselves. As one perceptive schoolboy put it:

> You can't just consider the cane by itself. It has to be understood as part of everything else—the whole process, the pressures, the emphasis on academics, the people downtown, your parents.
>
> JULY 1969

An Academic Image: Asset or Liability?

> In 1877, the teaching staff of Canterbury College decided that most of their students were deficient in knowledge of the subjects they proposed to offer for their degree courses. The staff therefore suggested to their Board of Governors that they might consider the expediency of establishing a Boys' High School . . .[2]

Thus set up as a "feeder" for what was to become the present University of Canterbury, Boys' High was given a pronounced academic orientation from the start. Its academic achievements over the years—especially in the area of school certification and university entrance pass rates[3]—frequently have been as successful as those of any school in New Zealand.[4]

[2] Douglas Cresswell, *Eight Christchurch Schools* (Christchurch, New Zealand: The Pegasus Press, 1956), p. 5.

[3] The School Certificate Examination conducted by the Department of Education is regarded as the accepted test of a completed secondary education for the great bulk of the pupils who do not desire to proceed to university. Normally it is taken in the Fifth Form year (15 years of age). The University Entrance Examination is conducted by the University Entrance Board and is the test taken by most pupils in becoming credited for entrance to a university. It is usually taken in the Sixth Form year (16 years of age). In actual practice, secondary schools can grant UE certification independently of the results of the UE examination.

[4] "Hard" data on examination results of schools purposely are kept confidential by the Department of Education. Nonetheless, it is generally acknowledged that

Establishing one's academic credentials in the eyes of the community marks the beginning of one's concerns and responsibilities, however, not the end of them. For a distinguished academic reputation usually demands a correspondingly distinguished (and continued) academic performance—that is, if one wishes to preserve one's hard-earned reputatin, an old rule with respect to which Boys' High is no exception.

As the Christchurch community has come to expect academic excellence of Boys' High School, most of the school's members have come to expect at least as much of themselves. The obligations and responsibilities of the participants in such a situation seldom are less than before; usually they are more, compounded by an examination-oriented syllabus which effects the content of teachers' subject matter, as well as the style of its presentation. If this means hard work for the faculty, it places just as heavy a burden on the boys. For as the "star performers," they are the ones who must ultimately produce. No one, boys least of all, can help but be affected by the stress on academics, much less by its two most regular attendants, the pressure to excel and a spirit of unrelenting competition.[5] Discussing the decision to send his son to Boys' High, one of the school's masters expressed his awareness of the situation this way:

> Now if he wasn't competitive, I don't know as I'd send him here. This is not the school for a struggling boy I'm afraid; at least that's the way it's presently set up, because of the academics, and because of the teachers. Even some masters treat the more poorly equipped boy by telling him he's an ignorant rascal. And when a boy gets enough of this all year he starts to realize he is not as bright as his classmates. Even the other boys get on to him and let him know that he's not very bright. I shouldn't think they would, but they are a bit this way.
>
> SEPTEMBER 1969

Others consider this spirit of academic competitiveness a desirable attribute. The following is a paraphrase of one master's response to the

---

Boys' High compares favorably with the "top" schools in New Zealand based on School Certificate and University Entrance Examination pass rates.

[5] In a comparison of New Zealand and Midwest American schoolchildren, Havighurst notes: "There is a striking difference in the frequency of mention of *Examinations* as a source of Fear. While this is only mentioned 1.2 percent of the time by New Zealand girls and .3 percent by New Zealand boys, this is more than ten times as frequent as such mentions by Midwest youth. This probably reflects the difference that school examinations play in the lives of the children in the two countries. New Zealand youth must pass a national examination to get the 'School Certificate,' while Midwest children can graduate from high school simply by passing their courses, and final examinations do not play such an important part in the outcome." Robert J. Havighurst, "A Comparison of New Zealand and American Children on Emotional Response and Moral Ideology," in Havighurst's *Studies of Children and Society in New Zealand* (Christchurch, New Zealand: Canterbury University College, Department of Education, 1954), Section VI, p. 11.

question, "What are some of the things that make your job an enjoyable one?":

> He especially liked the spirit of competitiveness that permeated the school, twice using the term "predatory" to characterize, in his judgment, the almost animal-like fierceness with which boys pounced on one opportunity after another. It was a trait that made itself most evident on the sporting field, he felt. But it was to be found as well in the area of academics.
>
> EXCERPT FROM FIELD NOTES, JULY 1969

The Boys

When Boys' High School opened its doors for the first time in 1881, it had an enrollment of 82 boys. By 1969, the year in which this study was conducted, the number of students had swelled to 1,093—128 in the Upper Sixth Form year (17 years of age), 253 in the lower Sixth Form (16 years), 241 in the Fifth Forms (15 years), 224 in the Fourth Forms (14 years), and 247 in the Third Forms (13 years).

The lads who eventually find their way to Boys' High, like most of New Zealand's schoolchildren, begin their education at about age 5. They pass through the infant classes (the "primers") and Standards 1, 2, 3, and 4. This normally takes six years. Being mostly city pupils, they probably then enroll in one of Christchurch's several intermediate schools, passing through Forms 1 and 2. Their training up to this point most likely has been coeducational. By now about 13 years of age, they are ready to enter high school. The next five years will see them complete Forms 3, 4, 5, Lower Sixth (16), and, except for a handful, Upper Sixth (U6). Boys' High annually accepts about 250 such boys, selected on a combined basis of academic ability, old boy ties, and geographic proximity to the school.

With the exception of four general course classes in the Fourth and Fifth Forms, most of the school's boys are streamed according to academic ability. Table 1 is a summary of the school's course offerings based on this division.

Classes average in size from 25 to 35 pupils, the largest being at the Third Form level. Overcrowding is a matter of especial concern to the staff, and stands out as another of the conditions influencing participant perspectives on corporal punishment:

> Third Form classes are sometimes as much as 36 in number. And these little fellows are just full of life. But the classes are so large that sometimes you've got to squash them a wee bit.
>
> MASTER, MAY 1969

The socio-economic distribution of the school's student population appears in Table 2. It is based on a division of the city of Christchurch

TABLE 1

TABLE 1
*1969 Course Offerings by Form and Stream**

Third Forms:
All Third Forms will have a common course consisting of English, French, Mathematics, General Science, History, Geography, in addition to the core subjects—Music, Art, Woodwork, and Physical Education.

Fourth and Fifth Forms:

Course†	Main Subjects	Other Subjects
A,B	English, Mathematics, Physics, History or Geography, French or German, Chemistry or Latin	Music, Art, Physical Education
N	English, Mathematics, Physics, Chemistry, Geography	History, Music, Art, Physical Education
G	Four classes—English, Mathematics, General Science; one from Geography or French or Commercial Practice; one from History or Commercial Practice or Technical Drawing	Music, Art, Physical Education

NOTE: (1) Classification of boys into the appropriate Fourth Form at the beginning of the second year will be based largely on such considerations as the pupils' performances and aptitudes as revealed in the Third Form. Parents' wishes and pupils' vocational needs and inclinations will also be taken into consideration. Entrants for the A,B classes will be selected by the school based on their academic ability.

(2) The content of these courses may be varied from time to time.

Sixth Forms:
The following subjects are taken at Sixth Form level: English, Latin, French, German, History, Geography, Mathematics, Mechanics, Physics, Chemistry, Biology, Book-keeping [sic], Economics.

* Source: Christchurch Boys' High School Prospectus for 1969, pp. 3–4.

† A, B, N & G refer to the various academic streams in which boys are placed at the beginning of the Fourth Form year. See Note: (1) above.

into eight census districts each of which is roughly socio-economically distinct.[6] Granted, there is likely to be some variation in the equation of socio-economic standing with geographic locale. Moreover, the physical

[6] Extreme differences in New Zealand between rich and poor do not exist as compared with a country like the United States. Relatively few people are found in the highest or lowest income categories. There are, however, notable differences in the size and range of income of various social groups, dependent largely on occupational status. Social strata also exist in New Zealand, distinguished by ". . . life chances, life style, and patterns of association. . . . The occupation position appears to be the dominant factor in the differentiation of social strata." See Cora Vellekoop, "Social Strata in New Zealand," in *Social Process in New Zealand,* edited by John Forster (Auckland, New Zealand: Longman Paul Ltd., 1969), pp. 233–71.

TABLE 2
Socio-Economic Distribution of the School Population
for the Academic Year 1969

| | *Socio-Economic Designation of Census Districts | | |
	"Fair"	"Good"	"Best"
Census district by zone number	6, 7	1, 2, 3, 8	4, 5
†Number of boys from each district	14	266	612
% of boys from each district	1%	30%	69%

* Advice as to the rating of residential areas was sought from University of Canterbury faculty knowledgeable of the city's socio-economic distribution. Differentiation was based on a composite estimate of income, type of occupation, type and quality of homes, and social standing of residents. Admittedly the terms "fair," "good," and "best," are imprecise designations. Moreover, they are based on individual opinion rather than "hard data." While Table 2 probably comes quite close to the mark, until it can be tested, it should be regarded as a rough approximation rather than a firm proposition.

† Total school enrollment: 1,093. Total number of boys counted: 1,033 (for the other 60, the attendance card was unavailable or the boy's geographic designation was in doubt, hence not used in the total). Of these 1,033, 141 were out-of-area attendants and could not be strictly classified. This left a total of 892 "in-town" boys on which to estimate the school's socio-economic makeup.

proximity of the school to districts 4 and 5, makes these areas the most logical from which to draw on pupils. Nonetheless, Table 2 clearly indicates that the boys who attend Boys' High come mainly from the higher socio-economic brackets in the Christchurch areas. Discounting out-of-area attendants and those whose attendance cards were not available for inclusion in the total, approximately 69 percent of the boys live in the so-called "best" areas, 30 percent come from "good" settings, and only 1 percent are drawn from the "fair" category. It is evidence of this kind which makes for the oft-heard suggestion that:

> Boys' High School really is an atypical state school with many of the characteristics of a private institution.
>
> MASTER, MARCH 1969

As part of the overall effort of this observer to experience life at the school from the perspectives of its members, a question usually asked of them was, "What are some of the things you like (and dislike) about this school?" It is worth noting some of the more frequent responses to this question. For the kinds of things which they claim to like or not to like about Boys' High say a great deal about what it means to be a boy of this school:

16

It's a good school; it's got a good name; you get a good education here . . . it's got a tradition . . . the teachers are of a good quality . . . it's considered that Boys' High is one of the better schools in the area . . . the compulsory sports . . . the way things are taught here . . . it means something to be able to say you've attended this school . . . the business advantages: if you apply for a job, and a boy from another school applies for the same job, you'll get the job . . . there's a great spirit here . . . the grounds are big and you can eat your lunch anywhere . . . there aren't any girls here; there would be too many distractions with them around; you work harder this way.

COLLECTED ASSORTMENT OF BOYS' LIKES

Some of the same items that appear on boys' list of likes reappear on their list of dislikes:

I'd rather like having girls around. I've always attended boys' schools. It's unnatural. I'll probably be a sex fiend by the time I leave here . . . wearing caps is one of the most ridiculous things I've ever encountered . . . some masters—I won't mention any names—have their own views on things; and if you don't agree, well . . . the furniture is too old; some of it is falling to bits . . . the Deputy Master; he's always trying to scare you . . . this school doesn't exist for the boys in it; the boys don't matter; this school is like a little computer . . . the traditions; they hold you back . . . some of our teachers aren't as good as they should be for a school of this kind . . . the uniforms; I think we should be like in American schools, where you can wear what you want . . . the way some masters cane first and ask questions later.

COLLECTED ASSORTMENTS OF BOYS' DISLIKES

The Masters

The masters who greeted the first boys to walk through the school's doors were only four in number, including the Headmaster and his First Assistant. Eighty-eight years later, the school's full-time staff had increased to 45 men. (Boys' High School is not quite an all-male institution. It has a school secretary, a librarian, a half-time mimeograph operator, and a quarter-time reading specialist, all of whom are female. It also has a large bust of Queen Victoria prominently on display in the school's main entranceway.)

The faculty at Boys' High works a Southern Hemisphere academic year, beginning early in February, and ending shortly before Christmas. The average teacher is 38 years old, has had 13 years of teaching experience—8 of which have been spent at Boys' High—prepares for 5 different subjects, and works 32 of a possible 35 periods each week. Together, the teachers can account for a total of 41 Bachelor's degrees, and 22 advanced degrees of one type or another.

Whether out of sentiment, for reasons of prestige, or both, roughly 30 percent of the staff are old boys of the school returned as masters. Whatever else their effect, the mere presence of such men constitutes a living, visible link with the school's past—not an unimportant consideration for an institution that places so high a value on tradition.

Up to 1968, Boys' High had had 50 masters with more than 10 years' service to the school, 27 with over 20 years', 14 with at least 30 years', and one with 43 years' service. Of the 14 who had been with the school for at least 30 years, 10 retired as recently as between 1956 and 1963. The unusually low turnover rate has been a mixed blessing, providing the school with a high degree of continuity and stability on the one hand, but with an equally high degree of conservatism and resistance to change on the other.

Masters' likes and dislikes are as much as indication of their definition of the situation as those of the boys:

> I enjoy the staff here enormously, no cliques, no factions . . . the boys; good quality, come from good homes, good to teach . . . the willingness of the Head to listen to my problems; I can go into his office, and I'll never come out without an answer . . . it's a boys' school; you can discipline a boy, whereas with girls there's nothing, absolutely nothing, you can do. A boy'll just say, "O.K. I've done something wrong, so thump me." But if you even bawl a girl out, she'll sulk . . . the school does not make a lot of demands on the teacher . . . the monitor system; [7] having to police these boys would drive me bloody mad . . . it's a happy ship; happy relations between boys and masters, and between masters and masters . . . no discipline problems here; the weight of the whole system is behind you; you can give a boy a detention, cane him, or send him to the Head . . . the tradition; it's a good thing; something you can look back on; without it this would be just another school.
>
> COLLECTED ASSORTMENT OF MASTERS' LIKES

Masters are less frequently complaining than boys, but equally vehement in their criticisms:

> It's damned smug; you see it in the staff, you see it in the boys . . . rulings from above; you can't reason with them, you just have to accept them . . . tradition; it gives the boys a sense of belonging, but it also obstructs change . . . the school's too big; we can't be as personal as we'd like to be . . . the boys—they're too loud . . . the school is out of

---

[7] The monitor system consists of 24 senior boys, including a Head and his Deputy, appointed by and responsible to the Headmaster. The monitors are mainly responsible for enforcing discipline among the other boys, particularly just before school begins, during the lunch break, and immediately after school. Masters are thus relieved of a good deal of the kind of extracurricular enforcement of order that might otherwise bring them into contact with boys on a less formal basis.

18

touch with the times . . . the false tradition; they build themselves up so much about what a great place this is and how terrific the boys are, when actually there's as much fighting and pilfering going on here as any school . . . there's absolutely nothing I dislike about this school.

COLLECTED ASSORTMENT OF MASTERS' DISLIKES

Relations Between Boys and Masters

The faculty and administration of Boys' High set almost all of the terms and conditions of the boys' activities during the course of the normal school day. Their control of what boys are to do, when they are to do it, something of how it is to be done, and what rewards and punishments will be given to those who abide or fail to abide by its standards, for most purposes, is complete. The basic relationship between most masters and boys may reasonably be called one of *subjection* and *submission*.[8] These terms are not used here to express an unfavorable judgment. Rather they are used as technical terms, out of reference to a largely authoritarian, hierarchical arrangement in which the masters, as the superior group, "call the shots." The masters, with good reason, believe that the arrangement is an appropriate one. They obviously know more about their subject matter than the boys, and have a much better idea of the kind of performance the school expects of its charges overall. Hence they are little inclined to share, much less surrender their power:

Once you start to give in to the boys, there's no stopping it. The tendency is to give in more and more. I will not allow that to happen here.

HEADMASTER, OCTOBER 1969

We don't like the idea of being dictated to by the boys—of having them tell us how to run things. We'll listen to their opinions in a reasonable way.

MASTER, MAY 1969

In the meantime, boys are expected to behave in accordance with the approved staff- and community-sponsored ideal of a "Boys' High boy." Table 3 specifies the rules and regulations with which the boys—incoming Third Form boys in particular—are expected to comply.

[8] In the same comparison of New Zealand and American schoolchildren earlier cited, Havighurst notes: "New Zealand children mention teachers about twice as often in Fear, Shame, and Sadness situations as Midwest children do. This probably reflects a greater frequency of punishment by teachers for New Zealand children, or perhaps a greater intensity of punishment. It may reflect the greater prevalence in New Zealand schools of corporal punishment. 'I was *sad* when I got the strap,' or 'I was *afraid* when I was going to get the strap,' were common responses for New Zealand children." Havighurst, *op. cit.*, Section VI, p. 13.

TABLE 3

Summary of School Rules*

A. School Property
1. There will be no skylarking or running in corridors.
2. Food scraps, waste-paper, ice-cream sticks or other rubbish will not be dropped anywhere other than in rubbish tins.
3. Articles left on top of lockers will be impounded.
4. Boys must keep off all corridor walls when waiting to go to class and when walking along corridors.
5. There will be no scribbling on, or defacing of, walls and furniture.

B. The Front Steps and main stairs are out of bounds for all but Upper Sixth Formers.

C. Bicycles
1. No boy will interfere with the bicycles of another.
2. All boys must dismount and walk their bicycles across the footpath at the Straven Road entrance.
3. Boys will cycle in single file when crossing Hagley Park and no more than two abreast when riding along roads.
4. Except for lunch boys, the bicycle area is out of bounds from 8:40 A.M. to 3:15 P.M.

D. Punctuality
1. Boys must be on the North (School) side of the river by 8:40 A.M.
2. Must be in room 2 minutes after first bell (or 2 minutes before second bell).

E. Uniform
1. Only the top button is to be left undone on flannel shirts.
2. Caps will be worn squarely on your head with no hair showing at the front. Cap must be worn with uniform, except if on motorcycle or driving car.
3. Socks will be no lower than two-thirds up the leg.
4. Singlets not to show about Grey Shirts.
5. Width of trousers to be 17 inches or above at cuff.

Ignorance of any school rule cannot be regarded as an excuse for its violation:
Haircuts—reasonable length, neat, sideburns not below line level with eyes; no hair below 1½ inches above eyes, or on collar.
Suit Coats—must be buttoned when worn.
Shorts—of reasonable length and reasonable fit.
Shoes—black school shoes with non-pointed toes.
White shirts—regulation white shirt without button-down collar.
Socks—grey or black coloured socks.
No hands in pockets.
Key rings—no unnecessary keys on the ring.
No playing cards at school.
No transistor radios at school.

* Taken from a copy of the rules read to incoming Third Form boys at the start of the school year.

20

Manners:
>Stand up when Headmaster or visitors come into room.
>Stand to attention when talking to master.
>Respect to masters when away from school.
>Raising cap, etc.
>No eating in the streets when in uniform.

No jewelry to be worn with school uniform.

No smoking while at school, in public or a public place, whether in school uniform or not; can smoke at home with parents' permission.

Exactly the same applies to alcohol.

School grounds:
>Must wear sandshoes or football boots on school grounds in winter term.

Buildings:
>Not allowed in Craddock Wing in lunch hour.
>Not allowed in Labs before master.
>Not allowed in rooms in lunch hour or interval, except in bad weather.

To be caught in violation of these rules usually is to pay a price. In order of increasing severity, youthful offenders are "warned," given a detention (written assignment or cleanup duty after school hours), or caned.

Irrespective of one's personal views, the fact is that the boys are a comparatively powerless collection of individuals. They may, on occasion, organize among themselves in an effort to influence the school's decision-making process. But their efforts meet with limited, if any, success when confronted with the powerful constraints laid down by the school's faculty and administration:

> Last year, in Fifth Form, I got 400 signatures in two days on a petition to abolish the wearing of caps. One of the masters told me a show of force was the wrong way to go about it. So I handed the matter over to the Head Monitor. He took it up with the Headmaster, who squelched it—didn't do a thing about it. You soon learn you have to conform to this system. Most of us are sitting University Entrance Exams this year, and next year we may be sitting bursaries and scholarships.[9] You don't want to rock the boat.

> LOWER SIXTH FORM BOY, JULY 1969.

[9] University bursaries consist of financial assistance to students. Bursaries available to graduating high school students are: (1) *fees bursaries,* which provide for payment of tuition fees, and (2) *fees and allowance bursaries,* which pay tuition fees plus a small allowance ranging from $80 in the first year to $200 in the fourth and subsequent years of the bursary. In addition, students may compete for the more lucrative University Junior Scholarships. These are awarded for a period of three to six years, depending on the student's program. They provide a scholarship allowance of $220 a year and are tenable with a fees and allowance bursary.

The relationship between most masters and boys can be further characterized as reserved, distant, and somewhat impersonal.[10] Their everyday encounters are not unlike those which might take place between an officer and his enlisted men, as indeed one master saw fit to point out:

> You have to keep your place, you see. That is, you don't want to be one of the boys; and the boys don't want you to be one of the boys. They want you to stay in your place. An officer doesn't go to the NCO mess unless he's invited.
>
> JUNE 1969

The boys may not entirely disagree with the preceding claim, but they do not entirely accept it either:

> "Some of the masters here are absolutely unapproachable," one boy offered. "That's right," piped in another. "You just don't get to know masters at this school as well as you did in the school I went to before. Tradition tends to keep you apart." By this time, it was the third boy's turn to say something. "It's not so bad as a Sixth Former. You've been here five years. By this time you have gotten to know some masters well enough. It's being in Third, Fourth, and Fifth Form that it's difficult."
>
> UPPER SIXTH FORM BOYS, JUNE 1969

The relationship is regularly acknowledged by boys addressing masters as "Sir," and masters, with few exceptions, addressing boys by their surnames. It would not take much to break the ice. But it is left to the master to take the first step. A few try:

> Mr. Smith calls us by our first initials—like P. J., C. A., and J. C. And instead of calling me Stevenson, he calls me Son of Steven, and I like that.
>
> THIRD FORM BOY, JUNE 1969

Apart from the fact that traditionally, "This is the way it's always been done here," the impersonality of the boy-master relationship is intensified by two factors: the overcrowding of some of the classes—especially at the lower levels and the combined insulatory effects of the staff room and the monitor system:

[10] Ausubel, in generally describing New Zealand secondary schools, states: "Still a third conspicuous feature is the wide social distance and the highly formal relationship between children and authority figures, rendering difficult any spontaneous and un-selfconscious exchange of ideas and feelings." David Ausubel, *The Fern and the Tiki: An American View of New Zealand National Character, Social Attitudes, and Race Relations* (New York: Holt, Rinehart & Winston, Inc., 1965), p. 86.

We're so out of touch with these boys. We don't know what goes on in their minds, what they're thinking about. They're like a bloody bunch of sheep being herded through the stalls. But it's the system that does this. If I only had 12 or so boys in my class. But 36. . . .

MASTER, JULY 1969

This staff room. That's one of my complaints. It tends to insulate you from the rest of the school. I've never seen a school where staff have no lunch duties. . . . I wanted to be able to meet some boys early when I came here. But I was told just to get my lessons prepared, to take one sport only, and to get settled in. It's pretty impersonal.

MASTER, JULY 1969

Conclusion

It was suggested in Chapter 1 that participant perspectives on corporal punishment would develop as an adjustment to and a reflection of the social and organizational pattern of which the phenomenon itself was an integral part, and moreover, that the existence of that pattern was possible only insofar as individuals could take one another's attitudes with reference to their activities and interactions and direct their behavior accordingly. This chapter has looked at certain features of that pattern, discussing some of the social and structural constraints that lead the participants to fashion their ideas and activities as they do.

Christchurch Boys' High, as has been pointed out, does not fit the familiar stereotype of the "average" high school. First, it is a boys' school. Second, it caters to pupils mostly from families of relatively high socio-economic standing. The kinds of students it has recruited, in conjunction with the kinds of obligations it has by virtue of its role in the community, have led it to adopt an organization that constrains faculty— and even more so, pupils—to place great emphasis on academic achievement. One result of this emphasis is an atmosphere of competition and pressures to excel. Furthermore, in keeping with its image as an institution of academic repute and standing, the school feels itself constrained to turn out not just a "good finished result," but a graduate that is clearly identifiable as a product of Christchurch Boys' High. It thus works to insure that its pupils conduct themselves in as strict accordance as possible with the staff/community-sponsored ideal of a "Boys' High boy." The perspectives of boys and masters generally toward one another and toward various features of the system arise in a relation of subjection and submission. The boy-master relationship, as a consequence, is mostly reserved, distant, and impersonal. The school itself is a "traditional" institution and is proud to be so regarded. Its past gives it a visible present and allegedly distinguishes it from other schools in the area. It

23

thus provides the school with a firm identity while simultaneously lending stability to its organization. Its only disadvantage is that it hinders change in the face of changing conditions.

Keeping in mind these features of the social and organizational milieu, the study turns now to "Caning: Educational Rite and Tradition."

Chapter 3

Caning: Educational Rite and Tradition

"Have you seen a caning yet, Joe?" I was asked by one of the younger masters. "Only once," I replied, "and that was Marty." "Ah," he intoned, partly for Marty's benefit, "he's one of our best. He has a certain style about him."

EXCERPT FROM FIELD NOTES, MAY 1969

To come to terms with the social meaning of caning at Boys' High is to catch something of the spirit with which the practice has flourished. It is not enough, in other words, to view the meaning of caning as a complex of the participants' ideas and actions. One has in addition to cultivate a "feel" for the manner in which the practice has portrayed itself over time.

The Making of an Institution: 1881 to the Present

To get at the significance of the current set of perspectives on caning at Boys' High is to go back to the founding of the school in 1881, and more specifically, to an incident involving the school's first headmaster, Thomas Miller.

Thomas Miller was an outstanding scholar "imported" from England in 1880 to head what was to be the first state-supported boys' school in Christchurch. Not a local man, Miller may have been out of touch with the rugged frontier spirit of nineteenth-century New Zealand. He was an "educational theorist" by New Zealand standards, a characterization which, in those days, even as now, was not always an advantage. His philosophy of education clearly was too modern for the times. For example, Miller laid down the rule that there should be no corporal punishment in the new school, a truly revolutionary measure which when put into effect ultimately led to Miller's resignation as Headmaster. As told by a senior master of the present school, the story of Miller's difficulties begins thusly:

25

Miller believed in no corporal punishment. He might have got away with that in England—their cloistered walls where persuasion would be efficacious. And he might get away with it the present day, although I doubt it. But he couldn't get away with it then. You see, the boys who might have been influenced by persuasion were already roped into Christ's College. The ones who were coming to Boys' High School were sons of workmen, rather of intelligence. But in addition to their intelligence, they were of a very tough quality, used to responding to challenges. And they were strong individualists. If they were to be made to submit to discipline, it needed a somewhat stronger physical hand—what Thomas Miller lacked. So he lasted two years; and then the Board of Governors of the school broke him—on the issue of corporal punishment and discipline.

APRIL 1969

Miller's resignation in 1883 was due fundamentally to a lack of definition of the Headmaster's jurisdiction and the extent of his responsibilities. There is little doubt, however, that Miller's anti-corporal punishment stand lay importantly at the heart of the controversy. The particulars surrounding the incident are noted in a biography of George Hogben, Thomas Miller's First Assistant:

In August 1883, a big stir was created in Christchurch, by the publication of a circular addressed "To the Governors of Canterbury College, and the parents and Guardians of Pupils attending the Boys' High School," in which Miller stated that he had offered his resignation on account of repeated interference by members of the Board. The reasons given for Miller's resignation appear rather trivial today. Two boys had climbed into the swimming baths at night; they were caught and, as punishment, asked to stay in on Saturday. Instead, the boys went to a cricket match and Miller then suspended both for the rest of the term. The parents wrote to the Chairman of the Board of Governors complaining of excessive punishment, and stated, in particular, that at any other school the boys would have received a severe beating which was all that was necessary in a case of that nature. The Board, in their reply, upheld the Headmaster's action, but as Miller's abolition of corporal punishment had never been popular with the Board, they did so in a lukewarm way, and there was some criticism at the Board meeting of Miller's methods of running a school.[1]

More than just another anecdote about corporal punishment, "the Thomas Miller incident" is a poignant introduction to a frequently recurring theme of the study: No one—not even a Headmaster the caliber of a Thomas Miller—ignores except at his peril the unspoken dictum of the school and its community that corporal punishment is part and parcel of the established order.

[1] Herbert Roth, *George Hogben, a Biography* (Wellington, New Zealand: New Zealand Council for Educational Research, Whitcombe & Tombs, Ltd., 1952), p. 20.

26

Inasmuch as Miller's brief tenure represents the only period in the school's history during which caning was not in vogue, one might rightly ask if his version of "moral suasion" was an effective alternative. Perhaps as reasonable an answer to that question as can be found comes from two old boys claiming firsthand acquaintance with Miller's methods:

> You must not suppose that he scolded me—I don't believe he ever scolded anyone; he simply asked me questions about myself, and talked to me until I felt what a worthless wretch I was to carry on as I had been doing; and I went out of the room resolving to be a regular pattern boy in the future; and so I was, sometimes, for a week or two, until that old fool ———— called me an idiot, or else I forgot to be good.[2]

> Miller was a perfect gentleman without any side; he always spoke quietly to me, but when he said it you knew you'd got to do it—you simply couldn't help yourself. I never knew anybody cheek him but once, and that was X. Miller simply looked at him, and I believe he was as miserable for the rest of the lesson as he had ever been in his life. He was more miserable afterwards when he got outside, for we gave it him pretty hot, I can tell you.[3]

George Hogben assessed Miller's application of "moral suasion" in these terms:

> Another innovation, still more strange to the ordinary mind, was the rule he laid down that there should be no corporal punishment in the school. This rule was due to his firm belief in the sweet reasonableness of boys, and if it is not given to all of us to attain to what seems like a counsel of perfection, he had no difficulty in following it himself, and a pedagogic experience of more than a quarter of a century enables me to say without hesitation, that he succeeded far better with what most people would consider a severe handicap than almost anyone else without it; the result with him was not merely the maintenance of order, but a moral discipline that entered deep down into the lives and hearts of the members of the school who came under his immediate personal influence.[4]

Thomas Miller's successor to the Headmastership in 1884 was the youngish, 29-year-old Charles Edmund Bevan-Brown. "Balbus,"—as Bevan-Brown came to be called [5]—handled the reins of the school for 36 years, becoming a legend in his own time.

[2] George Hogben, "In Memoriam: Notice to Thomas Miller," *Boys High School Magazine,* No. 19 (Term 1, 1901), p. 7.

[3] *Ibid.,* p. 7.

[4] *Ibid.,* p. 7.

[5] Taken from one of the sentences of a Latin Grammar Book—"Balbus built a wall," an honorific title pointing to Bevan-Brown as the man who built a school on the foundations laid by Thomas Miller.

If Thomas Miller indeed was out of touch with the spirit of early New Zealand, the same cannot be said of C. E. Bevan-Brown:

> Well now, the next Headmaster was superficially very similar to Mr. Miller, and had a very long reign. He suited, he fitted the atmosphere of Christchurch like a glove. He was ideal for the time, and for the temper of the age. Like Miller he was a very religious person. But he was more of a muscular Christian than Miller, and he swung a good hefty cane.

Pressed on all sides by the unease and ill feeling that had attended Miller's untimely departure, and which now threatened the school's survival, Bevan-Brown worked to put Boys' High back on its feet. Acting partly on the basis of personal philosophy, partly in response to community expectations, "Balbus," in one of his first moves to improve a deteriorating situation, replaced Miller's system of "moral suasion" with the method more in keeping with the "Kiwi" temperament. As Bevan-Brown tells it:

> In the school was soreness and upset, many boys being removed. Naturally his (Miller's) successor, a young man of 29, arriving amid this soreness and disquiet would find things somewhat difficult, especially as his experience of schools had not been lengthy. He was a new chum and would have to make his way. . . . The system of "moral suasion," which I found in vogue, was unsuited for any but rare spirits, and I had to introduce the *ultima ratio* of the more familiar method.[6]

Caning was not an exclusive Headmaster's privilege, however, except possibly during its earliest stages. Masters also could cane. Evidence of this comes from the recollection of an old boy who attended the school during the early 1890's:

> There was a boy in the lower First who day after day "left his exercises home," and day after day Mr. Alpers threatened that he would buy another cane; one day the boy come late, and was horror stricken to see that the cane was bought at last; he tremblingly explained that he had left his exercises at home, but would bring it next day; he did, but he did not escape.[7]

Until 1924, only those boyish misdemeanors deemed serious enough for consideration by the Headmaster were formally recorded, and then not in any masters' punishment book such as the one that is kept today. Boys' misdeeds at that time were entered instead in an impressive looking 400-page leather-bound volume with the letters "Appearing Book"

---

[6] Charles Edmund Bevan-Brown, "Recollections By the Headmaster," *Boys' High School Magazine,* No. 30 (1904), pp. 68–69.
[7] "Reminiscence of an Old Boy," *Boys' High School Magazine,* No. 30 (1904), pp. 68–69.

one supposes—still manage to find their way to the inner sanctums of the Headmaster's office, Bevan-Brown's old Appearing Book is no longer used to record their punishments. The last fleeting entry was in 1955: Melson, NS 3, Refused to obey monitor, Caned 4.

Conclusion

As Chapter 2 looked at the social and physical setting in which participant perspectives on corporal punishment develop, Chapter 3 has examined the latter's historical foundations. It has attempted to give the reader a "feel" for the color, the style, and the spirit in which corporal punishment at Boys High has flourished. It has suggested that the institution of corporal punishment at Boys' High has firm roots; that to understand the function and character of this institution is to understand the perspectives of its members; and finally, that to better comprehend the perspectives on corporal punishment of the present participants is to look as well at the ideas and actions of past participants.

The study moves now to a consideration of key perspectives and attendant patterns of action.

Chapter 4

The CIE/CIA Perspective:
Caning Is Expected/Caning Is Accepted

"I use it," he stated with reference to the cane. "I think you have to use it." "Why?" I asked simply. "Well, it's there. I mean it's used at this school. If you don't use it, boys think you're a softie. They'll tramp all over you." He paused, thought on what he had said, then concluded: "Yes. You're forced to use it. You really haven't any choice."

MASTER, MAY 1969

Caning Is Expected

As boys, masters, and parents interact with one another, they develop ideas toward various aspects of school life—ideas which, taken together, comprise a universe of discourse, a frame of reference in which communication occurs. In the process of this interaction, the participants create a variety of patterns of action, individual and collective, designed to enable them to cope with their everyday encounters with one another and with the school. Their actions grow out of their ideas and are extensions of them. Conversely, their ideas are influenced by their actions, the latter lending credence and meaning to the former as they assist in the creation of the kind of ordinary experiences which fit reasonably the situations to which they are applied. Considered collectively, the ideas and actions of the participants constitute a group perspective.

A key group perspective on corporal punishment at Boys' High is: Caning is expected.[1] Historically considered, the CIE perspective is the culmination of the school's traditional, unquestioning acceptance of corporal punishment, and is best understood as the embodiment of individuals' expectations of the cane in certain situations.

Seemingly intangible viewed merely as a concept, the CIE perspective is as real as a sledgehammer in its effects on those individuals falling under its influence. It is testimony to the existence and strength of this perspective that I noted it as an item of obvious significance within only three weeks of the study's initiation:

[1] This will be referred to as the CIE perspective.

I think of the first Headmaster—Thomas Miller—having resigned partly for his failure to condone corporal punishment. I feel the weight of 88 years in which caning has become as firmly entrenched here as it has. Small wonder how unmistakably strong is the view that practically shouts from the lengthy stone corridors, "Caning is expected." And I ask myself, "Am I exaggerating the significance of this perspective?" "No," comes the reply. Caning, in all its implications, is as real at Boys' High as Rugby. And nothing is more real at this highly sports-minded school than that.

EXCERPT FROM FIELD NOTES, APRIL 1969

The strength of the CIE perspective, however, stems not from the observations of an outsider. Rather, it is an outgrowth of the ideas and actions of the participants themselves. They are the ones who are affected by the perspective, and who, through their continuing adjustive responses to one another and to the system, bring that perspective to life, daily invigorating its status to a point that makes it difficult not to view the practice of caning at Boys' High as self-perpetuating.

Typical of the attitudes which sustain and are sustained by the CIE perspective is the response of a young new master in fielding the question, "How are you finding the students?":

"Oh, all right," he stated. "A bit noisy. I have a time keeping them under my thumb—especially Fourth Formers. They're in their second year. They're not scared any more. And they haven't got to sit for examinations 'till next year. So they're out for a good time I think." "How do you manage—as you say—to keep them under your thumb?" I asked. "Well, caning is the only way," he explained. "In some schools it isn't done. But in this school it's expected." "By whom?" I asked. "By everyone," he exclaimed, "the boys as well. They seem to expect it. They push you to the point where you almost have no choice. If you don't cane them they think something is wrong with you."

APRIL 1969

Asked, "How do you feel about caning?" a boy in the Fifth Form offered this opinion:

You expect it. If I do something wrong, it's only fair that I get caned. I think you respect the master more as a result.

JUNE 1969

Speaking as an old boy of the school, the parent of a Third Former had this to say about caning:

I approve of it, very definitely. I think it's very difficult for a lot of masters to control young boys without this. But it shouldn't be meted out

36

like candy—one or two boys get whacked—they'll know this master means business. It's infinitely better to have this form of punishment to give you stricter discipline. I can always remember masters who were so weak we had no interest—we didn't work. We did work, though, where we felt we had the threat of a whack. It's a fact of life at Boys' High.

SEPTEMBER 1969

Caning Is Accepted

It is one thing to expect the cane. It is another to accept it. The preceding quotations can be seen to contain elements both of expectance and acceptance. Distinguishing between these permits one to identify the second of the school's key perspectives on corporal punishment, *caning is accepted.*[2] Superficially similar to the CIE perspective, the CIA perspective can be mistakenly regarded as identical with it. But whereas both testify to caning's hallowed institutional standing, the first is significant of the expectations of the cane in certain situations, while the second attests to its acceptability as a fitting response to certain misdemeanors. The following exchange with the school's Headmaster typifies the sentiment of the CIA perspective. Moreover, it indicates that, with the exception of the "unjust" caning, corporal punishment is so accepted a part of the system that for all purposes it is not even an issue:

"Do you feel caning is effective?" I asked. "In this school, yes," he replied. "Why is that?" I pressed. "Because it's traditionally accepted in this school as a form of punishment. Period," he stated firmly. "How do you suppose the boys feel about it?" I inquired. "This I don't know," he said. "But this would happen. I would think that I would get information from this in discussion with the boys. As you know, I have these eighteen to twenty monitors—three times a year they come to me, in circumstances outside the school, where they just talk. I am sure that if caning was a worry to them, they would have told me. Mind you, monitors are a bit biased. But by the same token I think that I am sufficiently in touch with parents' and other people's judgments. Since I've been here, I've only had two parents ring me up about caning. On the one occasion, the parent accepted the caning as punishment for what happened, but thought I should know this boy had a physical deformity such that it wasn't wise for the boy to be caned. In the second instance, a master had made a wrong interpretation under the circumstances, and the parent was not really complaining at the broad issue, but simply letting me know that the boy was a bit upset about this; the parent felt an injustice had been committed, and asked if I could do something

[2] This will be referred to as the CIA perspective. With few exceptions, the participants simultaneously expect and accept the cane. The CIE and CIA perspectives thus work in tandem. They will be referred to in combination as "The CIE/CIA Perspective."

37

about it. Well, this was easily cleared up. I went and saw the master concerned. The master apologized to the boy for doing it. But these are the
only two complaints from parents that I've had in my ten years here."

MAY 1969

Speaking as if in support of the preceding remarks, a boy in the Sixth
Form stated:

It's not a case of bearing it. The usual sort of thing is that whenever you
get it you deserve it anyway. So why not have it? I can't remember getting a caning without a just cause.

SEPTEMBER 1969

Spreading the Gospel

One of the simplest, certainly more popular methods of perpetuating
the CIE/CIA perspective is storytelling. Regardless of whose ears various
anecdotes about caning fall on, their effect, if not always their intent,
is to legitimatize caning as an expected and accepted practice of the
school. To be sure, not all of the accounts one hears are meant even
indirectly to venerate caning's status. Some are calculated to have precisely the opposite effect. But these are definitely in the minority. Most
anecdotes are passed on in a good-natured manner which, besides add-
ing to the stockpile of colorful folklore, enforces the understanding that
caning is a significant part of what life at Boys' High is all about.

Old boys who on occasion address morning assemblies are not unknown to tell a tale or two about discipline in the "old days," and are
exemplary of the process by which storytelling invigorates caning's institutional standing. As the Headmaster explains the purpose of these
visits:

I invite these old boys to our assemblies from time to time as a way of
impressing upon the boys their heritage. The older old boys provide us
an important link with the old Worcester Street school.

APRIL 1969

Speaking briefly to the boys about " . . . what a wonderful heritage all
of you have to look back on," an 80-year-old graduate who attended the
school from 1902 to 1908 characteristically squeezed into his brief
presentation a lively recollection of his youthful rambunctiousness:

Now I don't want to give you boys an earbashing, but here's a story I
thought you might like. I was always getting into trouble of one sort or
another when I was a boy. One day I was told to report to the Head for

having gotten especially out of line. Well, I knew what was coming. So I got down to the lockers and slipped on an old pair of football pants under my regular trousers. Then I went into the Head's office. Old Balbus said, "Well, get your hands down in the usual position." I did. Then "Whack, whack!" and old Balbus was nearly smothered in dust. "You're incorrigible," he told me. "Get out of here." (Followed by hearty laughter all around.)

April 1969

Besides the well-intentioned stories passed from old boys to young boys, or which daily circulate among the boys themselves, there is the seemingly endless string of anecdotes which masters can be heard to exchange either over a quick cup of tea during the morning break, in the relaxed atmosphere of the lunch hour, or, as in the case of the following two stories, in the even more relaxed setting of Nancy's Pub—a favorite after-school haunt of the staff:

And then, Ian motioned me to come to the door and get a load of this. There was old Warren—enlightened educationist—tearing into a couple of boys with a vengeance. He looked so—so stately—with that white beard of his—almost like the Archbishop of Canterbury. (Laughter all around.)

Obviously having struck a responsive chord in his audience, and never one to be at a loss for a story, this particular master immediately followed up his first account with still another:

And do you recall so-and-so; he finally retired here at a ripe age a couple of years ago. I remember—it was his last year. He showed up in my office one afternoon—last period of the day, and said to me, "Alan told me there were some spare canes in your closet." Well, we looked and looked, but the only thing we could find was an old blackboard pointer, just about in splinters. He said, "Oh, that will do." He returned the pointer a little while later. "I know it's just silly," he told me, "a man of my age and experience—still caning. I walked all the way down here from upstairs to find one, and all the way back up again. But those boys just got to me so I couldn't take it any more." (More laughter all around.)

April 1969

The more serious implication of the preceding stories is clear: Whether one be enlightened educationist or experienced master, or both, caning is expected, caning is accepted, caning works. Ergo, caning is a fitting response to certain situations irrespective of who one is or what one otherwise stands for. Stories like these really are a way of saying: "If you really think you can buck the system, go ahead and try. And good

39

luck." They are an informal, yet powerfully effective reiteration of the twin perspectives that caning is both an expected and accepted condition of school life. The message, one suspects, is not lost on the several first-year staff who gather regularly at Nancy's to tip a jug or two with the older masters.

The Caning Books: Who Gets Caned for What, and How Much?

The Masters' Caning Book—certainly the one presently in use, but in all probability those of past years as well—is a most irregularly maintained set of records. The number of canings that actually occur are well in excess of those officially recorded, the latter finding their way into the Caning Book at random. Masters are aware of this fact, some of them to their chagrin:

> I don't think caning is controlled enough for younger teachers. I think we should be forced to put it in a punishment book. But I find the punishment book isn't used, because at the start of the year, I found that I had my name down a couple of times and there was hardly anyone else, and I know there were other people who were caning. So if you're going to have a punishment book it should be used, and the Head should use it to keep an eye on the younger teacher.
>
> SEPTEMBER 1969

Presuming randomness of entry, however, the caning books contain reasonable answers to the question posed in the title of this section: Who gets caned for what, and how much?

The last part of this question—how much caning goes on at Boys' High—is the more difficult to answer. The problem stems from (1) an incompletely kept set of punishment books, and (2) the impracticality as an observer of being witness to all of the school's canings. Using one of the few means of skirting these difficulties, I kept a record over an approximate five-month period of every caning witnessed in the normal course of everyday observations: In this way, a random sample of observed canings could be compared with the number of canings entered by masters in the Caning Book. Of a total of 20 caning incidents [3] witnessed, none was officially recorded. During that same period, however, a total of 38 other canings were recorded. Thus a more realistic appraisal of the number of canings that occurred over the period under consideration—presuming that *at least* 20 canings are unrecorded for every one that is—is in the neighborhood of 20 × 38, or 760 canings.

---

[3] A *caning incident* is defined as any misdemeanor entered in the caning book, and is counted as one incident irrespective of the number of boys involved.

This is an average of 5 caning incidents per school day. Admittedly this is a rough approximation and should be regarded as such. By the same token, these figures coincide with an estimate made earlier in the study solely on the basis of a "feel" for the situation that the frequency of canings averaged between 3 and 8 per day.

Whether this estimate constitutes a rise or a decline over the years is another matter still, one for which hard evidence, unfortunately, is even less readily forthcoming. According to the "old-timers"—the masters and old boys with vivid, if not objective recollections of the past—caning was simultaneously more frequently and more severely employed then than now. As one master put it, "Boys used to have their backsides warmed for so much as rolling their eyeballs in the wrong direction." In the absence of all but the flimsiest of facts, however, one accepts these claims with caution. Table 5 is a comparison of the total number of recorded caning incidents over a series of years.

TABLE 5

Number of Caning Incidents Recorded in Punishment Books

Year	1905	'06	'25	'26	'45	'46	'64	'65	'66	'67	'68	'69
Total Entries	68	84	63	96	142	169	269	153	138	104	37	76

In light of the probability that the variations from one year to the next are less an indication of a rise or decline in the use of the cane than they are a sign of the variability of masters' inclinations to officially record their canings, one is reluctant to credit (or discredit) old-timers' claims of greater frequency and severity of corporal punishment. One suspects, however, that masters in the early days of the school were neither more nor less discreet on the average than their modern counterparts; that the style and spirit in which caning is practiced has not changed appreciably over the years; and that proportionately it is used little more or less today than in the past. The following would appear to confirm the likelihood that the practice has not changed much—over the previous ten years, at least, if not over the last 88:

"Some people around here feel that caning is on the way out at Boys' High. Do you feel this is so?" I asked. "I don't think that this could ever be proven by statistics. There's a book in the staff room where masters are supposed to enter the names of the boys who've been caned and their punishment. Theoretically, I can't check if that's accurate or not, because if a caning goes on in the far corner of the place, I've no way of checking it. But put it this way. I'm not aware of a good deal of caning going on around the place. After all, boys are caned out in the corridor. And when they are, this place reverberates through and through. And you'd certainly know if there was a lot of it. I'm not aware of a great decline or a great increase. I would say it's the same as it was when I first came here ten years ago."

HEADMASTER, MAY 1969

What kind of offenses are likely to incur the cane as an expected, accepted response? In addressing oneself not only to this question, but to the related possibility that, qualitatively, such boyish misdemeanors as tend to invite masters' wrath have changed little over time, one looks at a sampling of offenses from the caning books over a period of 45 years. Table 6 consists of a collection of the first ten entries in the caning book for a given year, beginning with the year 1925 (the second year in which a Masters' Caning Book was kept), and continuing at five-year intervals until 1969. It includes a boy's form and academic stream (when noted), the nature of the offense, and in parentheses, the number of strokes received as punishment.

General impertinence, horseplay, disturbances in the corridors, talking—typically the kind of offenses inducing one to reflect that "boys will be boys"—these are the sort of misdemeanors which appear to have characterized the caning scene at Boys' High. Falling for the most part into one of two categories, they are the kind of offenses which either challenge a master's authority, or defy the unofficial commandment, "Thou shalt not rock the boat." They are the kind of transgressions which, if not properly dealt with, would turn a school upside down. Otherwise, they are not terribly serious misdeeds, at least not when compared with the grave problems associated with drug abuse, drinking, vandalism, racial strife, or the kind of complete disregard for authority that can be found at schools where the absence of discipline truly is a concern. Indeed, except for the lack of detailed explanation, one has difficulty differentiating qualitatively between the offenses contained in the Caning Books and most of the so-called "serious" offenses recorded in the Appearing Book (See Table 4). In short, the kind of difficulties that Boys' High boys appear to have gotten themselves into over the years not only appear to be relatively qualitatively constant, but are typically schoolboyish and comparatively trifling in nature. From the standpoint of the system, of course, one no more speaks of trifling offenses than one speaks of trifling rules. For all rules, being imposed from above, are to be obeyed implicitly.

42

TABLE 6
Caning Offenses at Boys' High School From 1925 to 1969

1925

3C   Cheating during test. Confessed quite openly on being questioned. (2)

3A   Talking after two warnings. (2)

3C   Continued neglect of homework. (2)

3F   Too frequent detention. (3)

3F   Too frequent detentions. Paper left on floor. (3)

4B   Taking chalk and throwing it at boys in class. (3)

L6   Struggling in Room H before my coming in. (2)

4C   Interfering with school chalk and writing on desks. (3)

4B   Given an extra hour for talking in detention. Failed to attend detention on Thursday and gave as excuse that he had been given permission to do the detention on following week. This was untrue. Given two hours to be done on Saturday. Failed to attend on Saturday. (4)

4B   Persistent neglect of work set. (—)*

1930

—   Interference with laboratory apparatus. (3)

—   Emitting untimely noise in class. (3)

—   Cheating in test. (4)

4B   Neglect of imposition. (3)

5R   Squared an hour's detention. (2)

4M   Continued neglect of work. (4)

—   Squared an hour's detention. (—)*

5M   Impudence. (—)*

5N   Releasing H_2S in room. (3)

—   Squared two detentions. (—)*

1935

—   Copying work, and lying when taxed with offense. Admitted. (4)

5A   Lying about misbehavior. (2)

3A   Lying when taxed with cheating. (—)*

3B   Causing trouble in singing by interfering with clothes of boy in throng. (2)

3A   Fooling on bicycles on main road. (2)

—   Detention squared. (—)*

5R   Continued misconduct. (2)

5R   Gross impertinence in class. (3)

5A   Continued interruptions. (2)

3C   Noise. (2)

1940

—   Throwing stones in baths enclosure. (2)

4GC   Doing imposition in class after warning. (2)

5GB   Causing deliberate disturbance in class. (2)

4PA   Reported by platoon commander for fooling at drill. (1)

3GA   Four detentions. (4)

4GB	Absent from P.T. without permission. (2)
4GC	Disgraceful work and slackness. (2)
—	Continued slovenly careless work after repeated warnings. (3)
5PB	Cheating. (4)
4PB	Impertinence. (3)

1945

3N	Misconduct in class. (2)
5GR	Misconduct. (3)
5GB	Chattering in class. (3)
4FS	Slamming door. (2)
5PR	In lieu of detention. (3)
4P2	Attempting a deception over lines. (2)
4P2	Horseplay. (—)*
4N2	Sent out from hall for misconduct during music period. (3)
3F2	Misconduct at physical training. (2)
5N	Singing in class. (—)*

1950

4FS	Neglect of duty. (2)
5L	Breach of contract. (2)
5N2	Impertinence. (3)
—	Lighting matches in class. (2)
4G	3 nights' science HW not done. (3)
5G	Fooling in hall. (2)
5N2	Corrections not done. (2)
3F1	Playing with rubber in suitcase during explanation. (2)
4FM	Inattention; imposition not done. (3)
4FM	Fooling at P.T. (2)

1955

4S2	Inattention; drawing on back of book. (2)
4N2	Flagrant disobedience. (1)
5L	Producing bad odours. (2)
3A2	Painting each other. (2)
5L	Fooling. (2)
5L	Childish behavior. (3)
5L	Disobedience. (2)
6L	Deliberate falsehood. (2)
4S1	Talking and inattention. (2)
4S3	Repeated neglect of work. (2)

1960

5R	Using excramentable language. (3)
5R	Gross verbal indiscretion. (4)
L6	Failure to report when sent for. (2)
—	Lack of work for test. (2)
5L	Disobedience. (2)
U6	Writing on board. (2)
—	Fooling and rude. (—)*
—	Untruthful. (—)*
4N2	Talking after 2 warnings. (3)
4N2	Forgetting detention twice. (2)

1965

	Insubordination. (3)
5R1	No homework or homework forgotten. (—)*
5N	Doing English in Maths period. (2)
—	No motorcycle registration and obviously absent from assembly many times—surly attitude to being questioned. (3)
5SW	Calling out. (2)
5SW	Talking. (1)
5SC	Causing trouble at tuckshop. (2)
5L	Not working with his violin as promised. (4)
3B1	Projecting projectiles. (2)
3B1	Idiotic behavior. (2)

1969

3B2	Talkative scapegoat. (1)
L6	Fighting in class. (2)
4B	Misbehaving in class. (3)
U6	Talking in assembly. (2)
5K	Failure to report for punishment. (3)
5J	General cheekiness. (1)
5J	Punching in class. (1)
5K	Repeated talking after warnings. (1)
4N	Cheek. (—)*
4N	Cheek. (—)*

* Information as to the number of strokes administered not in the caning book.

Table 6 having indicated the kinds of offenses for which a boy is likely to be caned, the question remains, "Who gets caned?" That is, which boys, differentiated according to form and academic ability, are most likely to find themselves in the kind of situations for which the cane is the likely response? Partly due to the difficulty of accurately ranking streams according to academic ability prior to 1950, but mostly out of a desire to present an up-to-date answer to the question of distribution, the figures of the following tables are drawn from the Caning Books for the period 1964 to 1969. Tables 7 and 8 note the distribution of caning offenses on the basis of form, while Tables 9 and 10 look at distribution based on academic ability.

Tables 7 and 8 illustrate what everyone at the school already knows, namely, Sixth Formers' relative immunity to the cane, a point to be discussed in the following chapter. Beyond that, the implication of these tables is surprisingly unremarkable. On the average, Fifth Formers— though not by much—are more frequently on the receiving end of the cane than Fourth Formers; the latter, in turn, are more frequently caned than Third Formers—but again, not by very much. However, the situation might as easily have seen the order of the distributions reversed, and viewing it strictly on a yearly basis—in particular 1964, 1966, 1968,

TABLE 7
Distribution of Caning Offenses* by Form, 1964–1969

Year	Total Incidents	Total Offenses	Percentage of caning offenses by form				
			3rd	4th	5th	L6th	U6th
1964	269	374	23	37	34	5	1
1965	153	266	20	24	52	2	2
1966	138	214	28	25	43	4	0
1967	104	146	19	37	42	1	1
1968	37	45	29	33	27	11	0
1969	76	114	35	34	18	10	3

* A *caning offense* is defined as any misdemeanor entered in the Caning Book, and is counted as one offense for every boy's name that appears in connection with it. The total number of caning offenses usually exceeds the total number of caning incidents in that frequently more than one boy is involved in a caning incident.

TABLE 8
Average Distribution by Form of Caning Offenses, 1964–1969

Form	3rd	4th	5th	L6th	U6th
Total Number of Caning Offenses	279	364	452	48	16
Percentage of Total	24	32	39	4	1

and 1969—does reveal a slight shakeup in the order of distribution. This suggests that no one of the lower three forms bears a disproportionate share of the caning load. In other words, Tables 7 and 8 imply that in recent years—Sixth Formers excepted—canings have been distributed on a comparatively even, nondiscriminatory basis.

Drawing from the same data used in Tables 7 and 8—Sixth Form boys excluded from consideration as nonsignificant—Tables 9 and 10 consider the question of distribution according to academic ability. Table 9 Indicates the raw number of caning offenses by form, academic stream, and year. Though there is a difference in the number of streams in the Third, Fourth, and Fifth Forms, the total populations of each form are, for all purposes, equivalent.[4] Table 10 divides each of the three forms into an upper, middle, and lower ability group in noting the average distribution of caning offenses based on academic ability for the period 1964–1969.

Whether looked at on a yearly basis, or as an average over all, the distribution of canings based on academic ability appears to be roughly even in the Third and Fifth forms, although the actual percentage of

[4] 241 in the Fifth Forms, 224 in the Fourth Forms, and 247 in the Third Forms.

TABLE 9
Raw Number of Caning Offenses Based on Academic Ability, 1964–1969

Stream†	1964			1965			1966			1967			1968*			1969*		
	3rd	4th	5th	3rd	4th	5th	3rd	4th	5th	3rd	4th	5th	3rd	4th	5th	3rd	4th	5th
1	8	7	21	4	2	8	12	1	0	6	0	3	7	3	2	5	5	1
2	3	9	18	0	0	10	7	3	3	0	1	1	1	0	5	9	7	0
3	12	10	16	21	17	14	1	22	4	3	4	20	1	3	0	15	6	4
4	13	31	7	11	15	16	22	2	16	9	14	6	2	1	1	4	3	2
5	30	37	13	3	3	6	15	8	4	3	8	4	1	4	0	5	10	6
6	18	34	12	15	19	20	3	9	15	7	15	11	1	1	3	2	3	2
7		12	5		6	15		9	13		12	3		3	1	0	5	3
8			17			29			27			5						2
9			20			21			9			8						

* Streams 4, 5, 6, and 7 are alphabetically rather than academically grouped for the Fourth Form in 1968 and 1969, and for the Fifth Form in 1969. Hence these figures are not used in the analysis of distribution based on academic ability in Table 10.
† Arranged in descending order of ability.

47

TABLE 10
*Average Distribution of Caning Offenses Based on Academic Ability,
1964–1969*

	Percentage of caning offenses within forms		
Ability Group	3d	4th	5th
Upper	28	13	29
Middle	37	43.5	30
Lower	35	43.5	41

canings declines slightly as academic ability goes up. Fourth Formers by comparison are in a class by themselves. The reasons for this will be examined in the next chapter.

Conclusion

Chapter 4 has identified a major participant perspective on corporal punishment in the form of the CIE/CIA perspective. This perspective reflects the point of view of boys, masters, and parents that they expect the cane in certain situations, and that they accept it for the most part as appropriate punishment.

The chapter also has suggested that canings occur regularly and relatively frequently at the school, that is, if one accepts an estimated five caning incidents per day as a measure of regular and frequent occurrence. Caning, as it presently is practiced at Boys' High, probably differs little from that of the past, though in the absence of firm information this claim is offered more in a context of speculation than certainty. The evidence of the various punishment books, however, in conjunction with historical references, suggests that the kind of offenses which incur a caning, as well as the style and frequency of the latter's administration, have remained relatively constant over the years. Furthermore, Sixth Formers excepted, canings appear to be comparatively evenly distributed among the boys, Tables 7-10 suggesting little, if any, discrimination on the basis of form or academic ability.

The next four chapters examine the perspectives on caning of the boys, the Headmaster and First Assistant, the masters, and the parents of boys.

"They cane you for such trivial things," Tony said. "Like what?" I asked. "Like talking, socks down, or putting your hands in your pockets," he explained. "One master," Elwyn added, "threatened to cane any boy who failed school cert. Well, some of these jokers aren't ever going to pass no matter how much they get caned. They should be given something useful like detentions and writing."

FIFTH FORM BOYS, JULY 1969

Boys are especially scornful of the master who resorts to corporal punishment out-of-hand. They even have a name for these types:

"Some of the masters around here are 'cane-happy.' They'll cane for absolutely nothing," he stated. "What do you mean by nothing?" I asked. "I'll give you an example," he answered. "Say Mr. Moss wanted to cane you. So he sent you to Mr. Watson to borrow his cane. Well, Mr. Watson would give you two of the cane himself before sending you back to Mr. Moss for two more." "Last year Mr. Watson showed up with a brand new cane," another lad piped in. "Why, he was so proud of it he even had two green ribbons tied to it. He must be nuts."

FIFTH FORM BOYS, JUNE 1969

No boy truly enjoys being caned. The practice thus carries with it the potential for escalatory response:

"As much as I sympathize with you fellows," I told them, "I sometimes get the impression you bring the cane upon yourselves. You practically ask for it." "Well, they (the masters) start it. They make the first move. And then you have to get back at them."

FOURTH FORM BOYS, APRIL 1969

Boys usually are at their most imaginative in "getting back" at masters. Good-natured exchanges occasionally degenerate into all out conflict. As in love and war, anything goes:

One of the boys came back at the end of the lunch break looking like the proverbial cat who had just swallowed the canary. "Boy, I can't wait 'till Mr. Lyndon goes to get his cane out of the closet," he proudly announced to his classmates. "Why's that?" I asked, smelling trouble. "Oh, he didn't show for the last class, so we ran his cane through the mangler," he proclaimed. "What's the mangler?" I inquired. "It's a machine we have in art class that you run things through and it crushes them flat." "I'm sure he'll love that," I offered. "You bet," Bob jumped in. "Last week we bent his cane at right angles and he didn't stop talking about it for the whole period." "Just why do you fellows do these things?" I asked innocently. "You just feel great," came the reply. "The chaps who do it are real big."

FOURTH FORM BOYS, MAY 1969

In the continuing struggle for classroom supremacy waged by masters and boys, it is essential to their "survival" that boys do not too frequently misjudge the limits of their tutors' tolerance. One has to know precisely where one stands. No one realizes this more than the boys themselves. Masters thus are classified according to their caning as well as their pedagogical capabilities. One learns from boys that so-and-so either is a "weak" caner, a "strong" caner, a "lousy" caner, or a "great" caner. Some teachers are known to give an impression of utmost seriousness while caning. Others are recognized for having all they can do to keep a straight face. There are one-handed caners, two-handed caners, left-to-right caners, and right-to-left caners. They come in all shapes and sizes. And the boys have every last one of them categorized:

> "You learn after a while that six of the cane from one master are worth three of another's or only one from a really good caner." "You mean to say you have the masters more or less ranked?" I asked. "That's right," and "Oh, yes," they all chimed in.
>
> FIFTH FORM BOYS, APRIL 1969

Because no two masters' policies on caning are exactly alike, boys must familiarize themselves with the particular stance of each of their superiors as soon as practically possible. The only reliable method of doing so—while at the same time keeping an accurate, up-to-date "file" —is to "push" one's tutor to the brink in order to ascertain precisely how far he will permit his charges to go. In addition to its tolerance-measuring function, "pushing" has the advantage of stabilizing via a process of ongoing definition an otherwise fluid, hence undesirable situation. One group of boys had this to say about "trying a new master out":

> First time he comes in the room, you wonder how far you can go with him. So you talk, and he says, "Stop talking;" so you talk again, and he says, "Stop talking." Well, then you can just go on talking. He should have come in and thumped the desk the first time good and loud, and then you'd know you're not going to talk in his class.
>
> FOURTH FORM BOY, JULY 1969

For others, all the way is the only way:

> If a master canes me then I know that's as far as I can push him. And I won't go that far next time.
>
> FIFTH FORM BOY, JUNE 1969

In the kind of situations in which the more imaginatively obstreperous youngsters drive their beleaguered tutors to cane, if not to drink, boys are not totally without sympathy:

Last year there was one master—a good bloke—who held mass canings for about fifteen boys every Friday at the end of school. But he was new then. He'd been working pretty hard. He was pretty exhausted by the end of the week. We'd been having him on, too. That's probably why he did it.

FIFTH FORM BOY, JUNE 1969

Their compassion may not be altogether consistent with their behavior, but it at least has a ring of sincerity. If that is consolation to some of the more harried masters, so be it. "Pushing," after all, is part of what the boy-master relationship is all about. "Everyone" knows it. So why not do it? Or that, at any rate, is the way the boys see it. "Pushing" is an acceptable, frequently fun-filled way of reaching a *modus vivendi* with one's superiors. Throughout, of course, the boys want their masters to be appropriately resolute. They may well decry the unapproachability of some masters on the one hand, but they will just as certainly deplore those who are indecisive on the other. In short, boys expect a firm hand, and are quick in their attempts to take advantage of weak or seemingly weak authority:

"You want to see a class where the teacher really hasn't any control?" John asked me. "Oh, it might be interesting," I replied. "But first tell me why it is that this particular teacher hasn't any control?" "Well," he intoned slowly, "he's too good." "What do you mean by that?" I asked. He explained himself. "Softhearted. He's too nice. He should be more strict."

FOURTH FORM BOY, APRIL 1969

Given the boys' reactions of skepticism, if not total disbelief, to the suggestion that schools elsewhere managed quite well without a system of corporal punishment, one has to conclude that a noncorporal punishment situation is beyond their powers of conception.

"Sir, may I ask you what teachers use in America if someone gets out of hand?" I explained that while corporal punishment was indeed used in some American schools, a verbal reprimand worked well enough in most cases, that detentions were also used, and that a student could be sent to the school principal and ultimately might face expulsion. "Oh, there has to be something more than that," he said incredulously. The rest of the group made it quite clear they did not believe me. Given the limits of their experience, they found it impossible to conceive of a workable noncorporal punishment situation.

FOURTH FORM BOYS, JUNE 1969

Indeed, boys are so thoroughly convinced of their own potential for unruliness that they consider themselves incapable of being reasoned with:

"Look," I said. "Suppose someone tries reasoning instead. Do you suppose the boys here could be reasoned with?" His answer didn't really come as a surprise. "They may listen to a teacher who reasons with them, but after he's through they laugh about it. They forget it pretty quick." Another lad summed up the group's feeling with the statement, "If you tried talking to a boy here it would just go in one ear and out the other."

SIXTH FORM BOYS, MAY 1969

In the highly male-oriented world of Boys' High, boys—when they do fall prey to the cane—are expected to take their punishment "like a man." In the parlance of the school, that means no whimpering, no excuses, no questions asked, no unnecessary show of emotion other than perhaps the stoic acknowledgment that the experience has been sufficiently painful. As a younger old boy put it:

When I was here, the feeling was to take it like a man. Be courageous. Let it be known that it hurt. But say nothing.

APRIL 1969

Pressing their claim to manhood as best they can under the circumstances, boys are inclined to equate the attainment of manhood with the overt display of masculinity. Thus, taking one's caning like a man means letting one's peers, if not one's teachers, know that one has the "guts" to withstand one, two, or if necessary, six of some irate master's best:

"It shows you've got guts if you can take it. The other boys all think you're kind of a hero," he said. "Why is that?" I pushed the point. "Well, they say, 'He took six of so-and-so's best. He's pretty good.' It's something he can run out and tell everyone about. It means he's pretty tough."

FIFTH FORM BOY, APRIL 1969

Caning thereby comes to signify status in one's peer group. One's social standing rises in proportion to the number of "notches" carved into his belt—one notch representing one caning. In this twentieth century of synthetics, however, boys sometimes are driven to alternative modes of display:

"When I asked them if it was really true that boys notched their belts for each caning, they eagerly replied, "Yes, yes." I then pushed the point, asking to see if such actually was the case. Warren was one of many to boast his belt for all to see. "But I don't see any notches," I said. "This is an elastic belt," he explained for my benefit, "so I have to make marks on it in ink." And sure enough, like bombing missions on the side of a B52, Warren had carefully inked in one slash for each of his canings for the first three months of the 1969 academic year. There must have been between nine and twelve of them.

FOURTH FORM BOYS, APRIL 1969

The belt-notching ritual normally is outgrown by the completion of the Fourth Form and is nonexistent in the Fifth and Sixth Forms. The reasons for this will be discussed later in this chapter. With the younger boys, however, it is acceptable, indeed desirable to visibly indicate one's solidarity with the group via an occasional caning. Not to have undergone this form of initiation is to risk the disesteem of one's peers:

> They call you a "goody-goody" if you've never been caned. You don't belong until then.

THIRD FORM BOY, MAY 1969

Confirming this, a former manager of the school's youth hostel noted the extent of peer pressures on "good boys":

> "If it was toward the end of the year and you hadn't been caned yet, you'd get the works," he said. "I don't quite follow you," I said. "I mean the other boys—they'd make you get caned," he went on, "like telling you to get out of bed after the lights were out and get caught so you'd have to be caned." "And you, as hostel manager, realized this was going on?" I asked. "Oh, of course," he replied.

AUGUST 1969

But as the number of notches on boys' belts soars skyward, the significance of the ritual changes correspondingly. Others begin to look askance at the hard-core belt notcher rather than in admiration of him. The "tough" guy is no longer the hero, though usually he is the last to realize it:

> "What kind of a boy is Jim?" I asked the others in order to ascertain the peer group standing of one of the more notorious belt notchers in the Third Form. "Oh, Jim's just a country boy . . . he came from the farm . . . not very bright," Bill offered. "Yes," Mike added, "when he first came here, everyone expected him to be pretty smart. He started off by always trying to answer lots of questions in class, but he never had the right answer." Doug jumped in with, "He got four of the cane from Mr. Norman yesterday. Mr. Norman threw a piece of chalk at him for talking, and Jim just threw it right back at him. There was nothing else Mr. Norman could do." "Now I suppose everyone knows who Jim is," I suggested. "Oh, everyone knows who he is all right," Mark agreed, "because he's always doing crazy things."

THIRD FORM BOYS, JULY 1969

55

Although the great bulk of boys mirror the perspectives on corporal punishment of their peers, a few march to a different drummer. They reflect the existing pattern only up to a point, going a step or two beyond their classmates in their assessments and in the sophistication of their views. While acknowledging the strength and existence of the CIE/CIA perspective, they indicate that they do not accept that perspective or they fail to behave entirely in accordance with it:

> I think that the student today is different from twenty or more years ago. Caning may have been all right then, but not today. It lowers everyone involved—master and student—to be laying into someone like that.
> FIFTH FORM BOY, APRIL 1969

And another:

> "Caning breaks down the relationship between teacher and pupil," Murray explained. "You can really get to hate the master who uses it. You want to get back at him any way you can." "It's archaic in this twentieth century," Mark piped in. John added, "Yes, it's absolutely barbaric, taking a kid out and bashing the hell out of him."
> FOURTH FORM BOYS, APRIL 1969

Different Perspectives for Different Reasons: The Breakdown by Forms

Third Form: These are the newcomers, the least privileged class, occupants of the lowest slot in the pecking order, the most impressionable of all the boys. For them life is an endless series of initiation rites, one set of obstacles after another—all in preparation for eventual acceptance into the fold. The unfailing object of the other boys' disaffection, no one—according to Third Formers at least—leads quite so miserable an existence as they do. Part of their problem is that they have yet to submit themselves completely to the faculty/community-sponsored image of a Boys' High boy. Third Formers are the least homogenized, most vital, certainly most energetic group of all. Dismal as life for the average Third Former might otherwise be, there is at least the future to look forward to—and a chance to get even:

> "Except for being glad to be here, there's not much pleasure in being a Third Former," one boy explained. "Yeah," another noted, "they call you 'tirds,' which isn't a very pleasant thing to be called." "It's tough," piped in still another, "Fourth Formers shove you around a lot." "Why?" I asked. "Oh, they're just through being Third Formers themselves, so they're going to get back at you," he explained. "Will you be any different as Fourth Formers, knowing what it's like?" I inquired. "Probably not," came the reply. "Do new boys in American schools get their heads

shoved under fountains?" I was asked. "Not usually," I answered. "We get that, and we get our knobs pulled off our caps. Last month I was left hanging by my belt on a coat hook in the locker room by some Fourth Formers. Once you're up there, you can't get down by yourself."

THIRD FORM BOYS, JULY 1969

Third Formers' perspectives on corporal punishment barely are in the process of development. They have had less time than the upper forms to take into account one another's attitudes and expectations, let alone those of the system. They have yet to abstract completely the school's desires of them. Consequently, their perspectives on caning are less consistent overall than those of the older, more adjusted boys.

Pressed on all sides by the need to prove and establish themselves, Third Formers are particularly responsive to the expectation that one take one's caning like a man. No one—Third Formers perhaps least of all—relishes being caned. But when the unwanted opportunity presents itself, Third Formers feel compelled to make the most of it, conducting themselves in a manner designed to eliminate any doubts as to their "toughness." In point of fact, most of them could not be more frightened. Whereas caning may be regarded as "ineffective" and "nothing but a big joke" to the older boys, it is anything but to Third Formers. Only subsequent to their baptism under fire, if then, are they able to assume the kind of nonchalant, devil-may-care attitude that they feel is expected of them:

> I asked them if they, like most of the older boys, thought caning was a big joke. "No, it's not a joke with us. It's pretty serious," a couple of them stated earnestly. "If someone else is getting caned, you might think it's funny," one suggested, "but you don't think it's so funny if it's you." "But afterwards it's kind of a joke," still another pointed out. "What do you mean?" I asked. "Oh, you joke about it. It means you're tough."

THIRD FORM BOYS, MAY 1969

If caning *is* an effective deterrent, however, this is the group on which it appears to exert its greatest influence. For with Third Formers, caning is a new, as yet untried experience. It usually is much worse in the imagination than in the flesh:

> As John explained it, he and several other boys one day forgot to bring to school a certain note signed by their parents. The First Assistant was furious, and announced that any boys not having the note in their possession after lunch would be caned by him personally. In John's own words: "Several of us lived too far from school to get home and back during the lunch break. So we reported to his office—all shaking in our boots. He had us in a line. Then he asked us for name, grade, and so on,

57

and told us one at a time to move over into the other corner of the office. By now we were all scared as the devil. Then he said—looking very stern—'I'm going to be lenient with you this time.' And he didn't cane us. He was just trying to scare the devil out of us." "And did it work?" I asked. "It sure did," he shot back.

THIRD FORM BOY, MAY 1969

Fourth Form: From a boy's standpoint, the Fourth Form year is the most desirable. The reasons are obvious:

Fourth Form is a good year to be. You've gotten used to this place. You know what's happening. You're not frightened as you were when you were a Third Former. In the Third Form you're new and so you work hard to impress. Fourth Form is a slack-off year, the year before school cert and U.E.'s.

FOURTH FORM BOY, APRIL 1969

Because they see this as the last responsibility-free year, Fourth Formers are the school's undisputed "hell-raisers." If any group is out to have masters on for the sheer fun of it, this is the group:

"Fourth Formers are the most cheeky. They give you the hardest time," Brent proudly announced. "You mean you purposely give masters a hard time?" I asked. "Sure," the rest of the group confidently replied.

FOURTH FORM BOYS, JULY 1969

Acknowledgedly out to enjoy themselves, they intend to make a show of it—for one another's benefit if no one else's. This is their way of visibly shedding the shackles of the previous year, of "bucking" the system that so far has held them in check. It is at the same time a convenient means of proclaiming their newly found in-group status and their superiority over the latest crop of Third Formers.

While it still is true generally that few boys seek a caning, as a group Fourth Formers come closer than any other to being the exception to this rule. Belt notching—as a visible symbol of one's claim to fame—tends to reach the zenith of its significance toward the middle of the Fourth Form year. Before the year is out—with the responsibilities of the Fifth Form year already breathing down their necks—some of the same boys who earlier boasted of their "cheekiness" begin to assume a posture more in keeping with the school's expectations of its charges:

In Fourth Form, you don't get disciplined as much as in Third Form, where you really have to toe the line. In Fourth Form they expect more of you . . . it's more like the university, where if you don't want an education then no one is going to make you learn. But if you insist on doing something absolutely stupid, naturally you can expect to be caned.

FOURTH FORM BOY, OCTOBER 1969

Fifth Form: Fifth Formers "know their way around," still behave in a somewhat cheeky manner, but are rapidly outgrowing their obstreperousness in the face of pending School Certificate and University Entrance examinations. Fifth Form year is thus a no-nonsense year. It is a time for serious work and settling down. Confronted with the first of a series of externally administered examinations—their futures allegedly hanging in the balance—Fifth Formers are beyond the younger boys interest in caning. For them, its meaning is not the same. Their concern with the cane actually is better described as a "nonconcern":

> It (the cane) is there. You don't really care with school cert and UE exams to think about. If you play up, you know you'll get it. It's as simple as that.
>
> FIFTH FORM BOY, JUNE 1969

Like most boys, Fifth Formers don't actively seek to be caned. But they do not go out of their way to avoid it either. Their attitude seems to be one of *"C'est la vie."* If it happens, it happens. And it frequently does. As Tables 9 and 10 have indicated, Fifth Formers tend to come under the cane at least as much as any other form. But for most of them, it hardly matters. If anyone regards caning as a big joke, it is the typical Fifth Former. They have been through this before; it is beneath their concern, beneath their level of maturity. The deterrent effect of the cane on the average Fifth Former is, at best, minimal.

Sixth Form: These are the bona-fide members of the establishment. More than any other group, they can be truly said to have seen it all. And they know it. The Sixth Form years are the years of arrival. These are the boys who have successfully hurdled most of the school's obstacles. They see themselves as something of an upper class, attendant privileges included. When the staff breaks for morning tea, most boys break for the four corners of the school. Sixth Form boys head for the sanctuary of the school's front steps. For them, the luxury of languishing there and taking exception to the rule that there shall be no eating at this location is indeed a privilege. For no one sits and eats food on the front steps of Boys' High. No one but Sixth Form boys, that is. Some of them have been waiting as long as four years for this.

Understandably, Sixth Formers tend to view much that goes on at the lower levels as childish and immature. This especially is the case with respect to the cane:

> "Some of the younger boys even hold competitions to see who can get the most canings," Melville noted with a certain air of disdain. "Yes," Errol emphasized, "when I was in Fourth Form, one boy had 300 canings in one year. I only had 40." "Do you still compete for canings?"

I asked. "No," he laughed, "it's mostly done in the Fourth Form, where it's the thing to do. We're grown out of that now."

SIXTH FORM BOYS, MAY 1969

Not only have they grown out of competing, they've grown out of caning. Well, almost grown out of it. As Tables 9 and 10 once again indicate, Sixth Form boys are relatively immune to corporal punishment. And with good reason. Having invested heavily in the system, there is little tendency, indeed little need, as one boy put it, to "rock the boat." There is nothing more to prove. They've challenged the system, had their share of masters on, taken their portion of canings, and passed their exams. Their relative immunity to corporal punishment is testimony to their belonging, an acknowledgment of their emergence as mature young males. Sixth Formers stand as living, visible proof of the school's *raison d'être*. Thus, when Sixth Formers do get caned, it usually is no joking matter, their occasional claims to the contrary notwithstanding. This is not because, as with Third Formers, the experience is a frightening one. With Sixth Form boys it is an absolute indignity, a direct slap at what it means to be a senior boy of this school:

> You don't normally get caned as a Sixth Former. Oh, it happens. But not very much. When it does, it's a bit degrading . . . if a Sixth Former gets caned, it's an humiliation. You don't expect this.

SIXTH FORM BOY, JULY 1969

No cause is just cause for the caning of Sixth Formers—Upper Sixth Form boys in particular. Or that, at any rate, is how the boys see it. According to them, their "club membership" ought to carry with it the right to an occasional indiscretion. Any master who thinks (and acts) differently reaps little other than their unbridled contempt:

> Any master who canes a Sixth Form boy has got to be some kind of a twit.

SIXTH FORM BOY, MAY 1969

Conclusion

It was suggested in Chapter 1 that the perspectives on corporal punishment created by the participants would be a reflection of, and an adjustment to, the structural constraints of their environment; that to alter these constraints would be to alter as well the perspectives which developed in relation to them. Nowhere is this point so aptly demonstrated as in the case of the boys. Certain of their perspectives on caning may reasonably be said to be common to all of them irrespective of age, academic ability, or form. Others of their views, having developed in response to distinctly differing attitudes, demands, and expectations, are characteristic only of certain groups, and even of groups within groups. While the requirements of the system, in other words, are sufficiently homogeneous to lead boys generally to adopt a common perspective toward corporal punishment, the system is at the same time sufficiently complex to lead them to develop distinctly differing points of view.

With respect to the perspectives on corporal punishment which boys hold in common, it has been shown that, with few exceptions, they expect and accept caning as an essential activity of the system, and object only when it is flagrantly excessive or applied with apparent partiality or for the wrong things. They prefer the cane to other forms of punishment because it is "quick," but simultaneously consider it ineffective, or at least less effective than detentions. They respect the "judicious" caner, but are scornful of the master who is "cane-happy." None of them enjoys being caned, but when punishment befalls, all feel obliged to accept it in stoic, "manly" fashion.

Looking at those respects in which their perspectives on caning differ, one notes the following. For boys in the Third and Fourth Forms, caning is a signification of peer standing and group solidarity, though in the case of the "hard-core" belt notcher it implies—to others, if not the individual concerned—failure to have coped successfully with the system's demands and expectations. It also is a serious, even frightening experience. This is less so as time wears on, caning loses its initial mystique, and initial fears change to philosophical acceptance and, eventually, relative unconcern. Fifth Formers bear proportionately as much and more of the caning load as any form, but express relative disinterest, given their greater concern with pending external examinations. For them, caning is "nothing but a big joke," doubtless as much an expression of their increased maturity as of their tendency to bravado. The Sixth Form boy is the culmination of the school's maturation process, hence he views corporal punishment with even greater disdain than the typical Fifth Former. For him, caning is significant of immaturity, a reminder of earlier struggles with the system, of adjustive responses to its demands, and at this stage of his existence, an unpardonable indignity.

Their differences of perspective and occasional disdain for caning notwithstanding, the statements and activities of the boys with respect to corporal punishment indicate that, individually and collectively, they accept and behave in accordance with the CIE/CIA perspective, and that the character of their behavior constantly invigorates that perspective so as to make it a significant feature of school life. The field notes yield a total of 50 items of evidence (i.e., discussions with boys, statements overheard, descriptions of incidents, and so forth) which stand in support of this claim, as against only 9 items indicating that boys do not accept or fail to act in accordance with the perspective.[1]

The perspectives which boys create in order to deal with corporal punishment are shaped by various influences—elders' expectations of manhood, the boy-master relationship of subjection and submission, the size and attendant impersonality of the system, pressures to conform, the emphasis on examinations and academic achievement, an atmosphere of competition, the inevitable process of maturation of the boys themselves, and more. This and preceding chapters have introduced these factors as underlying the social meaning of corporal punishment. It is for the remaining ones to bear out their significance.

[1] See Chapter 10 for a more complete treatment of evidence in support of the existence and acceptance of the CIE/CIA perspective.

Chapter 6

The Headmaster and First Assistant

Boys need discipline. That is why we corporal punish and all the rest around here.

HEADMASTER, MAY 1969

No satisfactory treatment of the study's problem can fail to note the influence of the Headmaster on school discipline. The reasons for this are aptly expressed in J. H. Murdoch's classic reference to the New Zealand principal:

> The form of discipline in the high school may, perhaps, be most concisely described in mathematical language as a function of two variables —the principal and the size and type of school. Of these, the principal is the more potent, for, if he will, he may resist the peculiar pressure of any particular type of school, and may even change that type. . . . The principal is the *fons et origo* of all discipline and beyond doubt sets the type and standard of the school control. He may rule alone, an autocrat feared by staff and pupils alike, respected, hated, or despised, as is the lot of dictators, but not really loved. He may rule, but in close cooperation with the staff, and staff meetings may really be conferences and not lectures. He may rule as a constitutional monarch throwing on staff and pupils the burden of discipline, and acting only in extreme cases. His personality, even where he keeps himself in the background, colours and affects all. The conception of school discipline held by the principal is, therefore, of the first importance.[1]

The concept of discipline of the school's present Headmaster could well be the subject of a study in itself, and no attempt to discuss it fully is made here. Rather it is the purpose of this chapter to provide the reader with some useful, albeit limited insights into the thinking of the Headmaster via a selection of the latter's own observations and assessments. The following excerpt is from a tape-recorded conversation with the Headmaster:

[1] J. H. Murdoch, *The High Schools of New Zealand, A Critical Survey* (Christchurch, New Zealand: Whitcombe and Tombs Ltd., New Zealand Council for Educational Research, Series No. 19, 1943), pp. 214, 219–20.

"Would you mind discussing with me briefly what you take to be your role as Headmaster?" I asked. As he explained it: "I think you accept the responsibility of the school. This is the main function. You have three main responsibilities. First of all the Board of Governors as the controlling authority. You then have a responsibility to the boys, to see that they reach an academic standard. Thirdly, you have a responsibility to the staff that does this. Lastly, of course, you have a responsibility to the parents. And this all sort of mixes in. . . . I took this school over as a first-class going concern. It was not run down; it was not in a bad state. The whole atmosphere of the place was excellent . . . so I just tried to continue on this sort of thing.

"From the boys' point of view, or rather in dealing with boys, it is understood by most headmasters that we are really *in loco parentis* . . . that our responsibility starts from the time the boy leaves for school from home until the time he gets back to home. As a typical case, I had a complaint from Sixth Formers this morning. Two of them came down to me and said we have a little Third Former in the bus who is not behaving himself; he's not showing courtesy to adults and we don't think this is right . . . this sort of responsibility outside of school."

What about caning?

"It can be abused; but if it is an accepted part of things, then it is viewed differently in the school than it is viewed from the outside, and this is what I don't think the outside public realizes. I have certain cut-and-dried things that are a caning offense. Now it is done without malice; it is done for no other purpose. But it is a form of punishment which accepts the level—same way if you're caught on a certain traffic charge, your license will be cancelled six months, and you go into it knowing that this is the situation. Now some of these things, for what they're worth, are childish, talked about in cold blood. But they're part of the system. We know that boys in New Zealand, as well as in other parts of the world, smoke. Alright, I'm not talking about it from a health stand-point; I'm talking about it from the attitude of the moral issue of the smoking . . . there are certain things you accept in a community as bad—sex, fights, and so on. But smoking is not on that level at all. But yet we say that because it's not accepted as anything a schoolchild would do in this community, if a boy is found smoking in a public place, he will get caned by me. . . . then you go further up the scale. If a boy is found taking a drink in a public place or anywhere it would bring disfavor upon the name of the school, then he is automatically suspended and dealt with by the Board of Governors. These things are cut-and-dried. . . . If a boy gets more than four detentions in a term, then I cane him. . . . I would be sure in this case there's no malice toward anybody. These are the majority of cases under which I cane. I never cane a boy under any circumstances except for school rules. I don't think I've ever done anything else but that since I've been here. So the amount of caning I do will depend entirely upon how many such cases arise or whether or not a boy has broken the school rules. And I would say that I might deal with three or four cases a fortnight. But my punishment in this way is simply because that is the established pattern in this school, and if they break it, they get punished."

Asked if he considered the offenses handled by him to be of a more serious nature, he replied, "I have to handle the ultimate . . . the other type of disciplinary problems we might have is with truancy, if a boy 'bunks' the school. Okay, we investigate the situation— bringing the parents into the situation. If the boy has deliberately 'bunked' without any real reason, any psychological point or anything like that, well, I deal with him in that way again. The other type of discipline is when masters get into the type of situation they can't get out of . . . and I'm always the ultimate adjudicator in these matters . . . a boy has the right of appealing against any punishment a master can give, and therefore they can come to me . . . and I would say you can always pick the masters who would do this. There's only about three or four of them who get themselves in an unfortunate situation where the boys appeal. . . . I never have dealings with any boys who are not doing their job in class-work; this is the master's responsibility. The ultimate sorts of punish-ment one creates on these—if you get the hard-core case of a boy not doing his work, lazy, the master's had him on, he's had detention, he's had him for extra work, he's still not doing his homework, parents are doing their best, still without success—this is not a punishable offense. I mean that this is not an offense at all for caning. First thing I do— I've got a couple coming in now—on what I call the '8:30 list'—they arrive at 8:30 on the dot with the homework they've done the night before, and they have to present it to me until such time as, frankly, I'm sick of it, or secondly that the message has got across. To my way of thinking, if a boy is reported to me for not doing his homework, can-ing doesn't meet the situation at all. This is a bit beyond that. I've got to go out and deal with the situation otherwise."

"My only worry on caning," he continued, "is that an injustice could be done to a boy by a master because he is trying to establish his own disci-pline. This is where caning is a worry. For a senior master around the school—one whose discipline problems never arise—well, he would probably meet his situation the same way as I meet my situation of caning—if a circumstance arises. But I would think that the vast major-ity of masters hardly ever use the cane. If they do, it's for something outside their own effect. For instance, if they walked down a corridor, and saw three boys damaging furniture in a room, they'd take them and cane them without any hesitation. But they'd never cane for something against the master himself because they don't need to. But when you get down to lower strata, this would be to me the only worry—where you get a new master in the place who has to establish his discipline. And it has again become traditional throughout the world, I suppose, certainly in New Zealand, where you have a new master on, and you give him hell, and this man has to react against it. Ultimately, in this particular situation, he feels he's got to establish authority by making an issue. And the issue will be a cane. And this would be, I think, the debatable grounds for corporal punishment."

MAY 1969

The following passage reflects some of the Headmaster's more deeply held convictions on the subject of discipline:

"You know, Joe," he said, "it's a funny thing, but it seems that a boy who has left this school, looking back upon his experiences, respects a former master most for one of two things. Either that master has given that boy a love for learning, or he has been the kind of master who has said, 'This is my opinion on this, and this is my opinion on that; this is where the line is drawn.' You see, a boy wants discipline; he wants rules. It's when a boy doesn't have this that he begins to feel insecurity."

JUNE 1969

Another passage supports the suggestion made in Chapter 3 that the application by the Headmaster of the "*ultima ratio*" invariably is tempered with an appropriate sprinkling of "moral suasion":

Without my raising the subject, the Head inadvertently supplied me with an interesting sequel to the four swishes of the cane I had heard coming from his office earlier in the day. We met by accident over a cup of tea and got on to discussing the complexities of any school situation—complex in terms of the personal makeup of each and every student and staff—complex as well in terms of the hundred and one daily decisions made in response to the school's activities. "Let me take an example of what I mean," he suggested. "One of the staff came to me to ask me to check into a situation where a boy had been repeatedly absent, allegedly because of sickness. The boy was out this morning, in fact, so we called his home. He came in this afternoon—on his bike—and reported to me. He apologized for having been out so much, but explained he'd been home sick. I said, 'Fine, but where were you this morning?' 'Oh, I wasn't feeling well,' he replied. 'Here's a note from my mother.' Well, I gave it no thought except to mention that I'd meant to look at the last excuse given by his mother. As I got it out of my desk, the boy became very emotionally upset. He suddenly said, 'I'm sorry, Sir.' Well, the two notes, as I then realized, were of two different handwritings. I then found out the real story. This boy is a golfer. He loves it. And he's going to be a good one. But this morning—and apparently a number of other mornings—he'd gone to the golf course, and just stayed there. So, what are you to do? You can't just say, 'Oh, well. I understand.' The boy had committed a flagrant violation." At that point, the Head gestured to me as to indicate the only possible follow-through—a caning. "And then I told him that the books would be closed on it from that point on, but to be more sensible next time and not let it happen again."

APRIL 1969

Nothing so influences the Headmaster's concept of discipline as his concern with instilling in a boy a proper appreciation of "the limits." Briefly explained, it is his view that there are, or if not, ought to be, hard limits to permissiveness, individuality, and freedom of expression:

"There are some things that people must learn to do whether they like it or not," he explained. "Take myself. Because of my position I can't even go into a pub—not that I necessarily want to anyway." He went on to express the suspicion that a good many of today's problems could be traced to overpermissiveness, that Greece and Rome fell from greatness in part because they were overpermissive; they allowed too many questions; they permitted too much philosophizing.

MAY 1969

And yet, wondering aloud about the youth's recent trend to irregularity of dress, the "sloppy, long-hair, barefooted types at the university," and their combined effect on boys moving on to post-secondary studies, he was moved to question the point of his own concern:

"I wonder sometimes . . . what's the use of some headmaster like myself insisting on these things at school (hair, dress, discipline) when they go to varsity and you see them like that." Describing a recent encounter with several "hippy" types at the university, he went on to say: "Granted, these were only a minority. But it makes you wonder . . . should we even allow free thought at the university. . . . I don't know . . . I just wonder . . . it worries me."

NOVEMBER 1969

His bewilderment about youthful behavior notwithstanding, the Headmaster's overall outlook strongly suggests that he sees more rather than fewer controls as the answer. On this point he stands firm, despite his acknowledgment that there are no "easy" answers to the more difficult problems:

This will interest you. Last week five boys were caught drinking. . . . I suspended them . . . but where do you take it from there. . . . I've got parents being brought in for talks with their sons before the Board of Governors and all . . . but where do you go from there? [2]

NOVEMBER 1969

The First Assistant

The First Assistant is the school's second-in-command. He serves as liaison between the Headmaster and the rest of the staff. His chief re-

[2] The sequel to that incident was not brought to my attention until long after I had left New Zealand: "Probably of more relevance to your work was the expulsion of five boys late last term. They took supplies of beer to the radio club hut and proceeded to get thoroughly tanked during the course of a school evening session devoted, ironically, to vocational guidance. Much evidence of the orgy remained and a staff sleuth reported to the Head." (Excerpt from a letter of September 15, 1970, written to me by one of the school's masters.)

sponsibilities lie in the area of administration and internal discipline. His influence on the latter is only slightly less than that of the Headmaster, and in some instances, more.

As at most schools, someone has to handle the system's accumulated "dirty work," the bulk of the disciplinary difficulties that are deemed serious enough for referral to some higher authority, yet not sufficiently dire to be sent all the way to the top. That man is the First Assistant. He is effectively charged with relieving the Headmaster of an otherwise burdensome disciplinary load. He thus fulfills the role in the eyes of most of the school's members—himself included—as the school's "number one disciplinarian." The following two excerpts provide some insight into the First Assistant's approach to his job:

> "Let me ask you what determines whether a misbehavior problem is referred to you as First Assistant, or dealt with by the teacher concerned?" I inquired. "That is a matter left entirely to the discretion of the staff," he replied. "And if the boy *is* sent to you?" I queried. "Well then," he answered with a slow smile, "I hand out my usual injustice."

> Without my inquiring further, he worked up to the topic of discipline. "I like this position, my dealings with the boys, even if some of them may hate my guts, if you know what I mean." "No," I pressed the point, "I'm not quite sure I know what you do mean." So he elaborated. "Perhaps a story will illustrate what I'm trying to say. A couple of weeks ago, while the Head was gone, there was a boy back at school. He had left school the day before—an Upper Sixth who decided not to sit for further exams and left school. Anyway, he'd been stopped by a master earlier that day and told his hair was a bit long and to tidy up. Well, the boy more or less told the master it was none of his business. The master told me about the incident. But the boy was already out of the building. So I went out and called him back. He was by now a block away, and off the school grounds. He was surprised I knew him by name. I had him step into my office. I said: 'Taylor, you haven't been a bad boy while you've been here. You've done nothing criminal. But you've gotten into your share of trouble. I'm going to do you a favor. I'm going to cane you. You'll leave this place feeling like all your debts have been paid. In five years' time you'll thank me for this. If you don't think this is right, of course, you're free to leave this office right now.' The boy thought it over and said to me, 'Thank you, Sir. You're right.' Now I get a great deal of pleasure out of that. Not the caning, mind you. That's incidental and unimportant. But I think the boys respect me. I try to be consistent. I try to be fair. I try to be sincere. I even don't mind a challenge from a boy on occasion. He can lean over the line a ways. But he'd better not step over it or God help him."

> APRIL 1969

By his own admission, the First Assistant's bark may be worse than his bite, and possibly a good deal more effective:

"Since you have brought up this topic of caning," I next asked, "I'd like to ask you what are your feelings about it." He paused for a moment, then said: "I find it most effective as a deterrent when it is used the least. I feel the same about capital punishment, incidentally. It's no good if it's used all the time. It loses its effectiveness. Frankly, I cane as little as I can. Ninety-nine out of 100 boys that come into my office walk out without getting the cane. But the point is, they leave me feeling they were lucky as hell to get out of here without one. I must confess, I do a bit of play-acting. I can get pretty grizzly. I'll tell a lad if he doesn't straighten up, I'll pin his ears to the front of my door, and he'll still be in there between them when I'm through."

APRIL 1969

Conclusion

Between them, the Headmaster and the First Assistant set the standard for much of what goes on at the school, as well as where, when, and how it occurs. Their influence thus extends to the furthest corners of the most distant classroom. Chapter 6 has attempted to give the reader an impression of the concept of discipline which lies at the heart of that influence. For insofar as the perspectives on corporal punishment of the participants develop in relation to the attitudes of others in the system, it is important that the reader appreciate the disciplinary attitudes of the system's two most influential "others."

The concepts of discipline held by the Headmaster and First Assistant reflect in part their individual "philosophies of life," in part the demands of their respective positions. Whereas the "Head," as the system's ultimate adjudicator, is prepared to see things in varying shades, the "First," as its "number one disciplinarian," is inclined to judge matters in "black and white." Their respective roles complement rather than conflict with one another, however, the one picking up where the other leaves off.

These differences of responsibility notwithstanding, their combined disciplinary stance simultaneously is a reflection and an enforcement of the authoritarian tone of the system. It is strict. It is rigid. It brooks no nonsense. It is reasonably consistent and impartial in its application and provides for precious little variation of conduct on the part of its objects. It is based on the assumption that "boys need discipline," and that proper discipline implies proper understanding of the limits of individuality, permissiveness, and freedom of expression. By the same token, their respective concepts of discipline spring from a deep, sincere, even paternal concern with boys' "best interests." In fairness to their more apparent authoritarian exteriors, the genuineness of the Headmaster's and First Assistant's concern for the boys' welfare is a point not to be minimized.

Finally, the ideas and actions of the system's two most influential participants indicate that they, too, accept and behave in accordance with the CIE/CIA perspective. Asked if he felt caning to be effective, the school's Headmaster replied simply, "In this school, yes." Further asked "Why?" he responded, "Because it's traditionally accepted in this school as a form of punishment. Period."

Chapter 7

The Masters: The Other End of the Cane

It was lunchtime. Bill casually announced, "Today I did my first real piece of teaching." "What did you do?" I asked, ready to play the part of the straight man. "I caned a boy," he answered with a big smirk on his face. "And what did he learn?" I asked. "He learned not to talk when I'm talking," Bill responded.

JUNE 1969

Most stories have at least two sides. This one is no exception. Whereas caning holds certain meanings for boys, it frequently holds entirely different meanings for masters. This is not surprising. Common sense suggests as much, as does the theory from which this study derives its rationale. To the extent that the ideas and actions of the participants arise in relation to differing demands and expectations, one expects boys and masters to develop differing perspectives in order to deal with corporal punishment under the various conditions of school life.

But the story is not as many-sided as one might suspect. Indeed, there is an almost surprising degree of agreement between the perspectives on corporal punishment of boys and masters, an indication that the constraints of the system are sufficiently generally applicable to all its members to engender considerable similarity of views between even so apparently contrasting sets of participants as those at opposite ends of a cane.

The CIE/CIA Perspective: Alive and Still Well

The ideas and actions of masters with respect to corporal punishment constitute an expression of overwhelming acceptance of the CIE/CIA perspective. Even those few who deviate from the majority point of view are realistic enough to accommodate themselves to this condition, and in so doing, tacitly support the status quo: [1]

[1] Masters usually were not asked directly whether or not they approved of corporal punishment. On the other hand, there was little doubt subsequent to my extensive encounters with them as to which masters accepted and approved of

Dave is one of those rare masters basically opposed to the use of corporal punishment under any circumstances. I can still recall his comment earlier in the year to the effect that he didn't use the cane and that some masters had let him know he was making their job difficult by not doing so. He takes his share of good-natured ribbing for his views, as was the case this morning when he quoted several passages from a psychology text during his free period. One of the staff present turned the quote around to suggest instead that more, not less repression was needed in the interests of the proper socialization of the youth. "So," Dave was half-seriously informed by his colleague, "you use the cane, and you'll be helping the modern generation." Momentarily sidestepping the latter's jab, Dave went on to note—mostly to himself— "There are some things in this book that really apply." This was quickly objected to with the retort, "But if some bloke is tearing you apart (referring to the boys' tendency to have a master on), who's going to feel better, you or him? What do you do then, eh?" Good-humored Dave, sensing the futility of it all, brought the "dialogue" to an appropriate end with the reply, "I guess I would have to hit him on the head with my psychology book."

Excerpt from field notes, June 1969

One might at least expect the members of the female set to take exception to the CIE/CIA perspective, or, if nothing else, to subscribe to another, possibly less virile approach to the disciplining of boys. The perspectives on caning of the handful of women at Boys' High, however, without exception, were indistinguishable from those of the men:

> "I would not want to see it go," she stated with reference to caning. Likening her experiences as a mother to the situation at the school, she went on to explain: "Well, little boys will just niggle, niggle, niggle. You can put them in bed for ten minutes, but that doesn't really stop it. What they want is a good smack to set them right. It's the same with boys when they go to high school—always trying to have a master on. They'll take their detentions, or they'll write their 100 lines. But it doesn't do any good. They need to be caned."

September 1969

Some Specific Perspectives

The particular constraints of the system have led masters to the adoption of a number of perspectives subsidiary to the CIE/CIA perspective. These may reasonably be seen either as extensions of the latter, or as strongly influenced by it.

---

corporal punishment and which did not. Of a total of 45 masters, only 5 expressed serious dissatisfaction with the practice, and a mere 2 indicated outright rejection of it under any circumstances.

applying the cane to their charges. Consistent with their own acceptance of the CIE/CIA perspective, for example, masters presume—with good reason—that boys both expect and accept the cane:

> "How do you suppose the boys feel about caning?" I asked. Repeating the view that I had heard from so many other masters, he said, "I think they accept it. They come here full knowing the cane is used at this school . . . mind you, I don't think they like it. You'd have to be a bloody masochist to enjoy it."
>
> JUNE 1969

Masters further feel that—the unjust caning excepted—boys accept the cane without resentment:

> I don't think there's any resentment, unless there's an injustice. And then the boys always have the right of appeal to the Headmaster. That, I believe, is the safety valve in the whole thing. But I don't think the boys really mind. . . . if they "bunk" school (play truant) they're going to get caned, and they know it.
>
> JUNE 1969

Masters see different boys as being differently affected by the cane. In remarking on the possibility of psychological damage, one master stressed the importance of sound judgment:

> You have to consider each case individually. A sensitive boy, a timorous boy—I won't cane. There you might do some harm.
>
> JUNE 1969

Furthermore, the effects of the cane are thought to differ not only from boy to boy, but from form to form:

> I think it really has an effect on Third Formers. They're impressed with all this. . . . it's a pretty scary thing for them to get caned. . . . it even has an effect on an Upper Sixth Former—his pride is hurt—he's been caned. But some of those hardened Fifth Formers—they don't care. They'll just say, "Go ahead and cane me. I don't care."
>
> JUNE 1969

Some masters know and believe in no other form of discipline. They state frankly that classroom control can be obtained only by the use of the cane and the fear that this engenders. Hence it is not uncommon for incoming Third Formers to be greeted in some of their classes by a master with a grammar book in one hand and a cane in the other. And to leave no doubt about his intention, the latter deliberately makes an example of the first boy unlucky enough to commit a trivial offense:

. . . caning works especially well with Third Formers. . . . it's important within the first two to three weeks that you single out one boy, the first one who gets the least out of line, and make an example of him. Poor little beggar—he has to pay. Who was it who said, "Better that one man pay wages for the sins of others. . . ." But it has to be done—otherwise you tell them, "The next time someone talks, I'll get the cane," and they say, "He'll never go and get it."

JUNE 1969

Consonant with Sixth Formers' view of themselves, masters acknowledge the relative "immunity" of the senior boys to caning:

I never cane a Sixth Former. I used to cane one of them occasionally—'till a headmaster told me "You could do that boy a great deal of psychological harm." And I knew this boy . . . and it could have done him a lot of harm . . . it's a difficult thing to judge . . . so I don't use it as much anymore as I used to . . . but I don't have to. I've had a fair amount of success with it in the past. . . . I still have quite a reputation.

AUGUST 1969

Just as a Sixth Former considers it an indignity to be caned by a master, a master considers it an indignity to have to cane a Sixth Former. Insofar as the senior boys symbolize much of what Boys' High stands for, a slap at a Sixth Former is a slap at the system:

"I don't cane Third Formers hardly at all—I give them a year to get their feet on the ground. Fourth Formers get caned more," he stated. "Why?" I asked. "A bit too adventurous," he replied. "Caning probably does Fourth Formers a lot of good. But if I have to cane a Sixth Form boy," he went on, "I'm embarrassed. If a Sixth Former puts me in a position where I have to cane him—and it's happened occasionally —I really do a job on him. I tell him, 'Here you want to be treated like an adult; you want to be able to walk into a pub and buy liquor; you're pressing for the vote; and you place me in a position where I have to treat you like a child.' Oh, I get mad."

JUNE 1969

In the masters' view, boys do not merely expect the cane passively. Rather, in what must seem to masters like an enemy's ceaseless probing of his opponent's defenses, boys are seen as actively pushing their tutors to the point where caning is the only alternative:

Now it isn't Sixth Formers that will give you trouble. It's the Third and Fourth Formers—the younger lads. If they detect the slightest weakness in you, they'll push you to pieces. They'll tramp all over you. And they'll not respect you one bit. They know it's something they shouldn't do. But they do it. And they know what they're doing. I have a son

78

who attends here. He told me about how hard a time one new master was having. He said, "It's unfair what we do to this new master." I maintain that if I cane, the boys have made me do it. I've had a boy tell me after he was given a long overdue caning, "You had to do it."

APRIL 1969

Small wonder that masters are at the same time victim and proponent of the attitude "You've got to be in there fighting all the time":

Hesitate for one moment and these boys will be right in there. . . . I'm not a terribly quick thinker, mind you, so it could be a problem. I guess you've got to be something of a bullshitter—take a stand and stick by it, even though you may sometimes be wrong.

APRIL 1969

Smaller wonder still that masters regard the Kiwi lad as "different," hence incapable of understanding anything but the cane:

Don went on to mention how he realized that caning wasn't generally accepted practice in America, but that it was necessary here because, "The New Zealander is a different kind of animal." The boys here, he thought, respected the judicious caner. They might not respect the abusive caner, but they held high the master who employed it justly. He even went so far as to suggest that boys might actually lack respect for the master who failed altogether to employ the cane.

EXCERPT FROM FIELD NOTES, MAY 1969

Without getting personal about it, the New Zealand boy is the kind of a lad who needs a jolt occasionally. Writing lines won't do it. Being talked to won't do it. The cane sometimes is the only way to break through to his mentality.

JULY 1969

Not unlike the boys who accept their canings as an expression of "manhood," masters view caning as a fitting, man-to-man way of dealing with boys. Discussing those things that made his job especially enjoyable, one master put it this way:

". . . the discipline here. You can cope with it . . . and you can deal with the boys in a man-to-man way," he noted with reference to caning.

JULY 1969

And another master, referring to boys' inclinations to visibly take their punishment "like a man," revealed something of himself as well:

I think taking a caning has something to do with semi-manhood.

JUNE 1969

79

The Plight of the First-Year Teacher: A Special Case˙

Nowhere is the strength of the CIE/CIA perspective so in evidence as in its effect on the inexperienced, fresh-out-of-training-college, first-year teacher. As an empirical confirmation of Mead's claim that, "That which creates . . . the various institutions in human society . . . is the capacity of the human individual to assume the organized attitude of the community toward himself as well as toward others," [2] the plight of the first-year master is worth special attention.

The master in his first year at Boys' High is confronted with many demands, not the least of which is his work load:

> I asked him what has become my standard opening question of first-year teachers: "How are things going?" "Tough," he replied, suddenly grateful for a sympathetic ear. "I must spend two to three hours every night preparing lessons," he told me. "How many different preparations have you?" I asked. "Five," he said. "It's a lot of work."
>
> APRIL 1969

Few first-year teachers come to Boys' High specifically with caning in mind. Fewer still fail to respond "appropriately" to the system's expectations concerning its employment:

> Before I came here I was behind anyone who said, "Do away with the cane" or "Caning has no place in education." But where it's accepted practice—as it is here—you accept it too. And because it's accepted, you find it's effective. Once you discover that, you tend to rely on it. You can get very accustomed to it—because you've found you can have an effect with it. Then it can get to be a habit. And that can be dangerous. You use it when you get emotionally upset. It's handy. You don't even think about it. You just say to yourself, "The cane."
>
> JULY 1969

The first-year teacher sees good reason to comply with the system's expectations on caning, namely, his responsibilities to his family and the unspoken dictum of the school that one either fits in or gets out:

> I have a family to consider. . . . also, it's this business of professionalism . . . if you're going to take teaching seriously, then you find yourself having to take the school seriously, too. You're going to have to conform.
>
> JULY 1969

[2] George Herbert Mead, *The Philosophy of the Act,* edited by Charles W. Morris (Chicago: University of Chicago Press, 1938), p. 625.

Confirming the validity of this concern, an older master noted of Boys' High:

> It's a pretty conservative place. Any newcomer had either better learn to conform or get out.
>
> MAY 1969

And as though peer pressures weren't enough to bring the first-year master into line, there are always the boys:

> Frankly, I'm against caning. But then there are these Third and Fourth Formers—always seeing how far they can get. And they expect it. If you don't cane them they think you're some kind of weakling. If I could rip into them verbally, it would be alright. But I tend to be unable to do that . . . I'm probably too serious. It would probably be better if I were at a school where caning weren't used.
>
> JUNE 1969

In the first-year teacher's sometimes frenzied efforts at establishing himself, anything goes, so long as it works:

> I asked him how he had found the adjustment to Boys' High last year as a new master. He said, "Not bad . . . I didn't have any real disciplinary problems last year. I was really lucky, I guess." "How do you mean?" I pressed the point. "Well," he continued, "with my bald head, most boys thought I was an experienced master. So they didn't push me. It wasn't until six months had passed that they discovered I was in my first year. Then it was too late."
>
> APRIL 1969

In addition to the "felt" pressures to adopt a fitting disciplinary posture, the first-year teacher is assisted in his adjustment by advice from others:

> "Well, how did you finally come to the decision to use the cane?" I asked. "I was at the pub one Friday after school with the rest of the staff," he explained, "and I was talking about how I was having a real tough time with some of my classes. They told me the only way to handle it was to give a few good canings."
>
> APRIL 1969

First-year teachers coming into the school as mid-year replacements provided useful opportunities for testing the immediacy of the CIE/CIA perspective's effects. As an outside observer I never ceased to be amazed at the speed with which newcomers, for all their reluctance, succumbed to its influence:

Possibly still another test of milieu influence has arrived in the person-age of Jim Mitchell, a replacement for one of the staff. This is his sec-ond day at the school. I spoke with him briefly in order to assess some of his disciplinary views before he could possibly have been appreciably influenced by the school's more predominant perspectives. I was already a bit late. "How are you finding the boys?" I asked. "Oh, they're okay," he replied. "Third Formers are quiet and innocent. Fifth Formers are a bit much; they think they're one up on everyone. You use a little sar-casm with them, and it puts them in their place. . . . I don't believe in corporal punishment. Oh, I'm not all that against it—it didn't leave any permanent scars on me. I just think it's ineffective." Just then, Alan Jackson, who knew Jim from university days, came over. "Alan tells me I'm going to have to belt some kid before too long," Jim noted jokingly. But from the tone of his remarks, it was clear he felt he could get along quite well without it. Time will tell, I muse to myself.

EXCERPT FROM FIELD NOTES, SEPTEMBER 1969

It did not take long for time to tell:

Precisely two weeks and two days after his arrival, Jim caned one of those "quiet, innocent" Third Formers. I confronted him with the inci-dent, particularly in light of his recent remarks: "I heard through Alan that you finally had to belt a Third Former after all," I said. "Yes," he laughed, "and unfortunately it worked. I still don't believe in it. But I have to admit it was effective. The class completely settled down after that—like they knew I meant business. It's mostly the expectation, I think. It's part of such a built-up thing here." [3]

OCTOBER 1969

The plight of the first-year master may be summarized as follows. He comes to Boys' High, usually fresh out of teachers' training college. His first impression of his job is that it is "tough." The work is hard, lesson plans are time-consuming, he is new, relatively inexperienced, and above all, uncertain, especially in the situation in which he is most vulnerable, the classroom. Pupils, sensing the slightest sign of indecisiveness as an invitation to battle, lose no time in putting him to the test. "Lesson plans, a new situation, the problems of adjustment, and now student insurrec-tions," he probably mutters to himself. "Who has the time to consider the alternatives?" For that matter, why bother when one is confronted

[3] An interesting sequel to this incident came my way 15 months later in the form of a letter from this same master, long since departed from Boys' High. One com-ment in particular points up still further the strength of the CIE/CIA perspective, while at the same time indicating that the perspectives on corporal punishment of the participants are a reflection of and an adjustment to the special constraints of one's environment: "Hearing from you revived my shame at having let the system get to me so quickly and thoroughly that I actually caned boys. Still, I did manage to resist a concerted campaign on the part of 5A to have me cane them!" (January 1971)

practically on all fronts by the only "acceptable" solution—caning. Students expect it. The staff leave no doubt that they expect it. Why fight a ready-made, time-tested, institutionalized, proved practice? "Caning it is," he tells himself, "at least until I get my feet on the ground; at least until I have established myself. Next year has got to be better, provided I last that long."

A Case Within a Case

Some beginning teachers adjust to the demands of the CIE/CIA perspective better than others, particularly if they are old boys returned as masters, full knowing what to expect of the system, and what the system expects of them. For these, the transition from disciplined boy to disciplining master is comparatively painless. For those less acquainted with the ways of the school, the change sometimes is nothing less than a major ordeal. The following is a presentation in three parts of one such individual's total adjustment to the system; it testifies once again to the existence and uncompromising influence of the CIE/CIA perspective:

I wanted to become acquainted with one of the new first-year teachers, inasmuch as I've gathered the impression that they, more than any other staff, have the greatest problems of adjustment. And so when I asked Larry Buller—a master in his first two months at Boys' High— "How are things going?" and Larry said, "I'm just swamped," I told myself, "Here is a likely candidate." This morning I visited Larry's first- and second-period classes. Afterwards we had a long talk about his job: "How do you find the boys, Larry?" I inquired. "Oh, they're not so bad now, though I really had a rough time the first couple of weeks," he said. I asked, "What do you mean?" "The boys started to get loud and unruly," he explained. "Pretty soon they were talking louder and more often than I was. I tried being friendly. I think that was part of my problem. That didn't work at all. They just got worse. But I finally got things back under control." "What did you finally do?" I asked. "Well, I finally had to cane some boys," Larry answered. "If you don't mind my asking," I inquired, "how do you feel about caning?" "Oh, I don't like to use it," he stated quite seriously. "I find it personally humiliating. In fact, the first time I used it, it was awful for me. I mean my hands were shaking. And you feel you're not doing a good job . . . I mean everything has fallen apart . . . you've lost control when you have to resort to caning. It's not a good feeling." "But you see," he went on, "it's that it's done here." "You mean it's almost as though you don't have a choice?" I asked. "That's right," he replied. "In some schools only the headmaster can cane. But here teachers can use it, and they do. Some masters overdo it." "Well, did your canings have any effect on the kids?" I asked; "I mean how did they take it?" "They were absolutely shocked," he said. "The trouble is, some of the biggest, liveliest bastards are the ones you like most. And you end up caning them, too. It's a bad thing. I don't like to do it." I note that Larry repeated the phrase, "I don't like to do it," at least a dozen times throughout the course of our exchange. He went on, "I caught one boy cheating on his homework and said, 'So, you're trying to put me on, you little bastard.' I really was furious at him, and I gave him two. Then, guilt feelings, I felt awful. I don't know. I've got to work something out." "How do you suppose the boys feel about it?" I asked. "Oh, they don't like it," he stated. "Why?" I asked. "Mostly because it hurts a hell of a lot," he explained. "I know I've hurt a kid or two with the cane." "Physically or emotionally?" I questioned. "No, physically," he told me, "although some of their backsides are so thick from caning that they're almost impervious to it." I asked if he thought the boys found it humiliating to be caned. "No, I don't think so," he answered. "I used to loathe being caned when I was a boy. Now I know what it feels like from both sides." "What didn't you like about it?" I asked. "It was the big sin," he stated, "the ultimate humiliation because only the headmaster administered it." "But you don't feel these boys are humiliated?" I asked once more. "No," he responded fairly certainly. "It's different here. It's just that"—and here Larry thought for a moment—"it's done here."

APRIL 1969

Larry's comments at the beginning of the school year frequently were emotion-filled. Obviously he was experiencing considerable difficulty in his adjustment to the system's demands and expectations of him with respect to corporal punishment. I was probably the first person at the school in whose presence he felt he could express himself uninhibitedly. Others might have construed his difficulties as a sign of weakness. As an outsider I constituted no such threat. I did not speak with him again on the subject of corporal punishment until three and one half months later. He sounded like a different person. The field notes catch something of the change:

> Not to my surprise, Larry appears to have made a considerable adjustment. His remarks, and in particular his tone and composure, were no longer indicative of the kind of inner struggles he had previously experienced. Whereas his former conversation was punctuated at least a dozen times with the almost plaintive cry, "I'll have to work it out," the substance of his remarks this morning indicated that in fact he had worked things out rather nicely. He has fallen in considerably more today than three months ago with "the party line." He still seems not to like caning. But three months under the influence of this particular milieu has had an appreciable calming effect on Larry's former lack of resolve: "I'm like most teachers," he stated confidently. "I don't like it, but I wouldn't want to see it go."

He spoke with decisiveness about the circumstances in which he would cane. He was still not completely in charge of the classroom. But he at least knew where he stood and what was expected of him: "I'll give a boy one cane stroke for talking . . . or take yesterday. Someone put a duster (chalk eraser) on top of the door so that when I walked in it fell down and hit me on the knocker. . . . I caned him twice. He won't do it again. If I had given him a detention he'd have hated my guts . . . they don't like detentions."

JULY 1969

By the final few weeks of school, Larry was speaking with the flourish and self-assurance of a seasoned veteran. The following is a fitting sequel to his initial struggles with the cane, his gradual resolution of the problem, and his final adaptation to the CIE/CIA perspective at the hands of the system:

> It was lunchtime. One of the staff was referring to a lad named Mc-Carthy—a young Fourth Former who'd apparently been asking for it, and got it, at Larry Buller's hands that morning. Responding to the one master's remarks, Larry—not lacking a certain pride about the whole thing, certainly not lacking in authority as he announced to all his achievement—put it quite simply: "I told him, 'McCarthy, you turn around once more and I'll smash you.' McCarthy turned around. So. . . ." Laughter all the way around, applause, appropriate number of bows taken, expectations fulfilled, only one curtain call, fini.

EXCERPT FROM FIELD NOTES, NOVEMBER 1969

Conclusion

As with the boys, masters' perspectives on caning are shaped by many factors: the pressures of conformity to the system, the emphasis on academic achievement and examinations, the ordinary day-to-day frustrations of teaching, the tendency of boys to "push" their tutors, the administrative inconvenience of alternative forms of punishment, the intensely masculine character of the school, the influence of tradition, But whereas boys are faced with a series of constraints that vary considerably from Third Form to Sixth Form—thus effecting changes over time with respect to the perspectives they create to deal with corporal punishment—the constraints placed upon masters—the first-year teacher possibly excepted—are roughly similar from one year to the next. Masters' perspectives on caning, as a result, are a great deal more homogeneous over the long run than those of their pupils.

Like the boys, masters prefer caning to other forms of punishment because it is quick, hence administratively convenient, an attitude which has led them to adopt the sub-perspective, "Caning is a nice thing to have around." Given the emphasis on academic achievement and the inevitable pressures which attend it—particularly during the week or two immediately preceding examinations—masters see the cane as a useful emotional as well as administrative convenience. To use one master's words, "It lets off steam." In view of its acknowledged all-round suitability, any master unthinking enough to seriously suggest the abolition of caning is given short shrift. Their various claims to the contrary, most masters reach for the cane first, in preference to detentions. The effort to be consistent with the generally accepted notion that one canes only for "serious offenses," combined with the recognition that the cane's effectiveness decreases in proportion to the amount of its use, leads masters to subscribe almost unanimously to the "I only cane as a last resort" syndrome. In further justifying their employment of so potentially brutal a punishment as caning, they have developed an attendant perspective to the "last resort" syndrome, "I don't really get any pleasure out of the cane, but I wouldn't want to see it go." In point of fact, this is just another way of saying that irrespective of its apparent barbaric overtones, caning is an integral, time-honored, hence legitimate practice of this institution. The masculine tone of the school, in conjunction with the physical aggressiveness which it engenders, leads masters to adopt the view that caning is an appropriately man-to-man way of dealing with obstreperous youngsters, hence all the more acceptable by everyone concerned. The tendency of the boys to "push" their tutors both reflects and enforces this state of affairs. Under these circumstances, it is important that a master establish his classroom standing immediately. For he knows that indecisiveness is an invitation to chaos. Some masters thus start off the school year by laying a cane on their desk and asserting that they know how to use it. And to show the class forthwith that they mean business, they purposely make an early example of the first hapless lad to step the slightest bit out of line. The participant-observer in these situations senses not so much a call to learning as a call to arms. The Kiwi lad may be, as some masters indicate, "a different kind of animal," given his inclination to physical aggressiveness and his apparent imperviousness to any form of punishment other than the cane. However, the basis of this claim has to be seen for what it is—not as a bio-genetic peculiarity, as some masters come close to suggesting, but rather as a culturally acquired trait, and furthermore, as an indication of the capacity of boys to take into consideration the attitudes of others toward them and to adjust their own conduct accordingly. While no two masters' policies on caning are exactly alike, they are reasonably consistent with regard to the kind of offenses leading to the cane's employment. Insofar as one can judge, most masters—the first-year master and the so-called "cane-happy" master excepted—are reasonably judicious with respect to the use of the cane. Provided they do not get caught up in the heat of the moment, as in fact they frequently do, most masters cane (or attempt to cane) with a view to the personality and temperament of the boy as well as the circumstances of his offense.

As a group, masters are even more overwhelmingly acceptive of the CIE/CIA perspective than boys. The field notes yielded a total of 115 items of evidence indicating that masters accept and behave in accordance with the perspective and only 9 instances in which they do not. This compares with 50 such positive items and 9 negative items in the case of the boys.

The perspective on corporal punishment created by the masters are undeniably collective in character. Clearly, masters do not come to hold this or that view of corporal punishment simply as a result of their own individual feelings and beliefs. Rather they arrive at judgments that are consistent, if not identical with the collective assessments of their colleagues. The plight of the first-year teacher generally—and the case of Larry Buller in particular—are striking illustrations of this point. They show that the perspectives on corporal punishment of the masters, no differently than those of the boys, develop as a result of their capacity to assume the organized attitude of the school community and to adjust their own behavior accordingly. For clearly, none of these first-year teachers came to Boys' High with the firm idea in mind to cane. Indeed, they indicated an opposite intention, only to find that "friendliness" was no substitute for firmness. That they rapidly acceded to the demands of the system indicates that the masters' perspectives on caning are no less collective in character than those of the boys, and that their ideas and actions stem less from the personalities of individuals than from the collective inclinations of the group.

Chapter 8

Beyond Boys' High:
The Organized Attitude of the Larger Community

> The cane? I'm all for it. In fact, I don't think there's enough of it. If there was more, there'd be fewer problems with kids today, don't you think? [1]
>
> MOTHER OF A SIXTH FORM BOY, SEPTEMBER 1969

This chapter looks at some of the attitudes of a community inclusive of, yet external to Boys' High School. It does this via a consideration of: (1) the attitudes and expectations of parents of boys at the school, (2) the interactions of this observer with New Zealand society at large, and (3) others' analyses of the New Zealand national character. It is an attempt to get at the character of the larger social context in relation to which the perspectives on corporal punishment of the school's participants have been created. It is based on the assumption that these perspectives have developed not only with a view to the demands and expectations of the school per se, but as an adjustive response to the organized attitude of a much larger community.

Getting at the Larger Picture

I did not cease playing my role as participant-observer merely upon calling it a day at the school. As a foreigner trying to fathom the ways of a strange country, I was in a real sense a participant-observer a good part of my waking hours—that is to say, my interest generally in the New Zealand way of life complemented my research interests. Important clues to puzzling aspects of caning presented themselves on innumerable, sporadic occasions during the course of day-to-day living. Bits of activi-

---

[1] Ausubel notes, ". . . the most commonly voiced complaint and apology of New Zealand parents is that discipline is no longer what it used to be and that laxness is undermining the foundations of both school and family life." David Ausubel, *The Fern and the Tiki: An American View of New Zealand National Character, Social Attitudes, and Race Relations* (New York: Holt, Rinehart & Winston, Inc., 1965), p. 86.

ties here, pieces of conversation there, the experience of shopping at the grocer, purchasing a car, teaching a tutorial at the university, belonging to the local ski club, socializing with a variety of "Kiwis" in all kinds of situations, familiarizing oneself with the currency of the language ("She'll be right, mate"), noting elders' attitudes and behavior toward the youth (and youth's attitude and behavior toward their elders), observing male-female relationships in various circumstances, visiting other schools in the area, and even being stranded by a snow storm for four days high in the Southern Alps with two old boys and their wives—all of these experiences served as an indispensable backdrop for the study's central problem.[2]

The following three excerpts are examples of the kind of spontaneous activities which in some cases suggested working hypotheses, and in others confirmed them. The first is typical of the many situations outside the school which generated testable hypotheses. The second exemplifies the kind of volunteered commentary which shed light on the character and organized attitude of the larger community. The third is characteristic of the innumerable, colorful references to corporal punishment which, taken together, underscore its social significance:

1. Earlier today I discussed with a university faculty member my suspicions regarding belt-notching as a signification of peer-group standing. Responding to my comments, he suggested that I further consider caning in its relationship to manliness. Referring to his own schoolboy experiences, he recalled a motto inscribed on the school wall: "Manliness is true virtue." His implication might well take the form of the following hypothesis: "To take one's caning in 'manly' fashion is in itself an indication of one's manhood." The suggestion that boys' aspirations to manhood are connected with the social meaning of caning is a point I shall not want to forget. For to even partly understand this phenomenon of caning is to cultivate an appreciation of the larger societal context of which caning is merely a part. And the more I reflect upon it, the more the social significance of manliness appears to be importantly bound up with the social meaning of caning at Boys' High.

MAY 1969

2. Last week I met with the editor of a leading educational journal. He raised a point which turned out to be of interest to the study:

[2] I mention these activities not to indicate that I enjoyed my stay in New Zealand —though that is not to be denied—but rather to point out that my participation in life "Down-Under" was both intensively active and widespread in scope, and provided me with a significant appreciation of the influence on Boys' High of a society external to it. No account of the study's problem would have been complete without the advantage of these experiences.

"It may be of interest to you that back in the 'fifties' Christchurch was the first of our large cities in New Zealand where gangs of youths began getting together—rebelling and causing mischief—like breaking up the piecart in the square. . . . I couldn't help but sympathize with some of these young people to a point." "How do you mean?" I asked. "Christchurch is a rather conservative city," he explained. "In some ways these youngsters had a good deal to be rebellious about."

That same afternoon, in a comment related to this, an associate of a leading educational research organization volunteered the observation that Christchurch schools traditionally had been far more conservative than schools throughout the rest of New Zealand. Part of the explanation, he felt, lay in the absence of appreciable teacher mobility. Teachers in the Christchurch area, he claimed—especially at the post-primary level—frequently remained at a school for as long as 35 to 40 years. Basically conservative, they tended to obstruct change in the face of changed conditions.

SEPTEMBER 1969

3. Max is a good friend, an inveterate story teller, and quite by coincidence, an old boy of the school. He has a habit of reminiscing about the "old days," and in particular about some of his experiences as a youth at Boys' High. One such experience, hardly to my surprise, involved the cane. As Max told it: "I'll never forget the time that old Jones and myself got caught poaching trout behind the cricket sheds at school." "What happened?" I asked obligingly. "Well, you see, it was a pretty serious thing, so we had to appear before the Headmaster. He had the two of us in, scared as we were, and do you know what that old bloke did? First, he read us a passage from *The Complete Angler,* a classic on trout fishing. And then he had us bend over and gave us a hell of a bloody good hiding." Pausing a moment to think on that one, Max then added the clincher. "Ya know," he mused with grinning self-satisfaction, "I still poach trout. Only I use bigger and better methods. No more of that hook and line stuff. Now I dynamite them."

OCTOBER 1969

The Parents

In an effort to supplement my random encounters with New Zealand society at large, I interviewed the parents of 20 boys of the school.[3]

As measured against the nearly 1,100 sets of parents connected with the school, this is not a sizeable figure. From a statistical standpoint, it borders on the insignificant. The parents interviewed, however, were not looked upon as a "sample" as that term is usually understood. Rather

[3] See methodological appendix for a discussion of my handling of parental interviews.

they were treated as a complement to the study, a useful indication—and possibly no more than that—of the attitudes of the larger school community. As it turned out, parental perspectives exhibited an almost incredible degree of homogeneity and consistency—enough so that despite the seeming insignificance of their numbers, one cannot but regard their collected statements as a reasonable indicator of parental perspective as a whole. The field notes acknowledge the point:

> Most of what Mr. and Mrs. Campbell had to say differed little from much of what the past 15 sets of parents had to say. Their remarks bear repeating, however, partly for the record, but more importantly because they testify to the consistency and relative homogeneity of parental thinking.[4]
>
> EXCERPT FROM FIELD NOTES, OCTOBER 1969

Indeed, the independently expressed attitudes of parents were so decidedly consistent that, at about the three-quarter point of the interview schedule, I found myself able to forecast their views with considerable accuracy:

> With only five interviews to go, I note that there is an unusually high degree of consistency to parental thinking. Their perspectives on education generally, and on such related items as the wearing of uniforms, the proper length of hair, the stress on academic achievement, feelings toward co-ed schools, and not least, the practice of corporal punishment, form a reasonably solid pattern—so much so that I find myself able to predict with perhaps 90 percent accuracy parental views on most educational topics.
>
> EXCERPT FROM FIELD NOTES, NOVEMBER 1969

[4] The homogeneity of the New Zealand people has been commented on elsewhere. Sinclair notes: "The European New Zealanders are a remarkably homogeneous people. An American journalist a few years ago caused great annoyance by writing that they all looked alike; but in comparison with Americans, they do. Men and women generally wear clothes conspicuous only for their dowdiness. They mostly speak alike. If we ignore the Maoris, customs differ little from one locality to another. This homogeneity is due partly to the predominantly British origins of New Zealanders, partly to the rapid development of communications in the past century, partly to the state education of the vast majority of the population." Keith Sinclair, *A History of New Zealand* (London: Penguin Books, 1959), pp. 276–77.

Mitchell carries the case for homogeneity a step further with the suggestion that New Zealanders are considerably uniform of thought and attitude as well. Looking at the results of a poll on the political leanings of the Christchurch population, he notes: "When the Christchurch sample were asked whether they ever thought of themselves as being to the left, the right or the centre in politics, just over half said they thought in these terms. Among them the great majority, like actors on stage, chose the centre. The finding that the electorate was not characterized by any ideological gulfs, but rather by a considerable uniformity of thought and attitude, also reflects the nature of New Zealand society and politics." Austin Mitchell, *Politics and People in New Zealand* (Christchurch, New Zealand: Whitcombe and Tombs Ltd., 1969), p. 191.

The average age of the mothers and fathers interviewed was 45 and 49 years respectively. Of the 20 mothers, 17 had a Fifth Form education or less, 1 had completed Sixth Form and 2 held a B.A. degree. Of the fathers, 10 had a Fifth Form education or less, 5 had completed Sixth Form, 3 had from 1 to 4 years' university experience, and 2 held post-graduate degrees. With the exception of one mother, all were native New Zealanders. The socio-economic standing of parents was judged on a combined basis of father's occupation, related probable income, residential locale, and the apparent quality of home and household furnishings. Utilizing the same descriptive categories applied to the Christchurch census districts in Table 2 (See Chapter 2), the 20 sets of parents are roughly socio-economically classified as follows: 3 fall into the "fair" category, 8 reflect "good" situations, and 9 reflect "best" situations.

"Why Boys' High?"

Parents' stated reasons for sending their sons to Boys' High are significant indicators of their expectations of the school.

It is clear from their response to the question, "Why did you decide to send your son to Boys' High?" that parents see Boys' High—as compared with other schools in the area—as offering certain "advantages." First there is the education:

> I believe a boy must have a good education if he's to get on in life. . . . I sent Allen to Boys' High because I heard it was a good school . . . I'd even go so far as to say it was the best secondary school in New Zealand. As I tell Allen, the education is there. If he doesn't get an education it's his own fault.
>
> FATHER, SEPTEMBER 1969

In addition to a concern for its purely educational advantages, parents indicated that there is considerable prestige attached to getting one's son into Boys' High:

> Boys' High has always been regarded as the premier secondary school . . . most parents would want their boys to go there if they could . . . the age, the tradition, the name behind it. Most people would get their boy in there by hook or crook if they could.
>
> FATHER, OCTOBER 1969

> Everyone seems proud to get their boy in there. . . . Mr. Morton down the street was absolutely furious at not getting his boy in.
>
> MOTHER, OCTOBER 1969

A concern with status and standing would appear to be only a part of the reason behind the desire to get one's son admitted to Boys' High.

Of at least equal importance are the perceived advantages which accrue to a boy subsequent to graduation:

> In Christchurch, Boys' High has got a good standing . . . for their future careers, for employment. In Christchurch they've got a far better chance going to Boys' High than any other school . . . it's an actual fact.
> FATHER, OCTOBER 1969

Still another reason for sending one's son to Boys' High has to do with the preference for a single-sex school and the advantages—real or imagined—of an all-male institution (i.e., "no fooling around," the absence of distractions from the opposite sex, and not least, man-to-man contacts): [5]

> "I agree with single-sex schools—don't like co-ed schools," Mrs. Martin stated. "Why not?" I asked. "Less distractions there," she explained. ". . . boys interested in girls, girls interested in boys at that age. It's best they get on with their education. Social life can get on later." "Do you really think this assessment of yours is correct—that boys would be all that distracted by girls?" I pressed. At that point, Mr. Martin—speaking in the dual capacity of an old boy—jumped good-naturedly to his wife's defense. "I think they feel more like men at a boys' school," he offered. "Nothing pansy about Boys' High. . . . take the Army. Now what would it be like if there were a lot of women in the Army?" he asked. "Is Boys' High like the Army?" I asked. "It's almost like the Army, I sometimes think," he answered with a chuckle.
> MOTHER AND FATHER, OCTOBER 1969

Consistent, perhaps, with the reputation of Christchurch as the "most English city outside England," the unadulterated love of tradition also plays a crucial role in parents' preference for Boys' High:

> It has a tradition—which seems to appeal to parents. I suppose this begins with the building itself—it's a rather pleasant place to look at—

[5] In his note on the social boundaries separating male and female roles in New Zealand, Gilson sheds some light on parents' preference for a single sex school: ". . . the boundaries separating male and female roles from those common to both sexes have altered over time, in response to changing social conditions and attitudes; but it appears that New Zealand has retained a more clear-cut separation than many other industrialized societies. Various features of its socio-economic system testify to the continued acceptance of traditional lines of separation. . . . There must be a social reason for a more extensive separation of male and female roles than is biologically necessary, and Parson's theory that it serves as a mechanism for reducing friction between the sexes in society generally, and the family in particular, undoubtedly applies in the New Zealand situation." M. Gilson, "Women in Employment," in *Social Process in New Zealand,* edited by John Forster (Auckland, New Zealand: Longman Paul Ltd., 1969), p. 189.

it has a sort of standing to say you went to Christchurch Boys' High. It has a standing throughout the country. This can't be said of all schools throughout New Zealand.

MOTHER, SEPTEMBER 1969

My eldest boy tells me tradition is what's holding Boys' High back. Other schools, the boys say, have a modern outlook. But I ask them, "How do you know? You haven't been to these other schools." Being a bit of a square, I personally value tradition—things that are substantial—things proven to be good in one's experience. I don't know. I'm a bit of a conservative. Perhaps it's an adherence to conservatism. I favor the British monarchy. I'm not ashamed of being proud of tradition . . . there is still this sort of upper crustish thing about Boys' High, and I don't know as you should try to diminish it.[6]

FATHER, SEPTEMBER 1969

A Highly Supportive Disciplinary Context

Parents generally claim little knowledge of the school's affairs apart from what they hear through their sons. Theirs is an unquestioned faith in the school's ability to do its best by their boy, and an attendant disinclination to "interfere" in its administration. Masters are seen by them as *in loco parentis,* and given a free rein. The immunity of Boys' High to parental criticism, for all purposes, is complete. Given the perceived advantages of attendance there, given their view of it as "the best," parents are reluctant to find serious fault with it. Boys' High, after all, gets results. For better or worse, parents are ready to accept what it has to offer *in toto*:

> "We never interfere," Mrs. Elton stated. "That's one thing we've never done is go to the school complaining about this or that." Confirming his wife's feelings, Mr. Elton added, "Neither of us have had any complaints. I figure they know what they're doing better than I do."
>
> MOTHER AND FATHER, NOVEMBER 1969

---

[6] Conservatism is still another feature of the New Zealand national character. Sinclair acknowledges the point: "The New Zealanders are usually a conservative people . . . not in the sense that they believe in unrestricted capitalism and rich men's governments, for the electorate is probably to the left of that in any English-speaking country, but in the sense that they usually resist change." Keith Sinclair, *op. cit.,* p. 279.

Mitchell again goes a step further than Sinclair: "This is not Burkean conservatism fearing to change lest organic growth be disturbed. Nor is it stand-pat conservatism. It is a far more genuine and potent form, the conservatism of the unthinking and untroubled man. Whatever is is right, at least if it poses no problems and causes no trouble. . . . Conservatism is the unspoken, inarticulate assumption of unchallenged man in a state of contentment." Austin Mitchell, *op. cit.,* pp. 194, 309.

Discipline is a matter of prime concern among parents. This is not to suggest that they consider discipline a problem at Boys' High, but rather that an emphasis on discipline is a major theme of their philosophy of child-rearing and education. Not surprisingly, parents expressed whole-hearted support for the regulatory policies and practices of the school:

> "The discipline there is much better than at some of these other schools . . . this is a very strict school," Mrs. Thompson noted. "So what's so wonderful about a strict school?" I pushed in an effort to get her to elaborate her views. "The young people today need stricter control," she stated. "Some of them get away with jolly murder at other schools." "For example?" I questioned. "I'll give you an example," she replied gamely. "Boys' High is noted for its politeness. . . . or if boys are caught riding three abreast on a bicycle, watch out. It's either an hour's detention or a caning. You hear of boys at other schools sassing masters back. That doesn't happen at Boys' High."
>
> MOTHER, OCTOBER 1969

Speaking on cadets—a one-week military training period at the start of the school year in which all but Third Form boys participate—still another set of parents expressed their concern with the need for discipline in this way:

> "Cadets, I think, is a very good thing there," she offered. "Excellent discipline, and discipline is what they need at this age. I'd never want to see cadets done away with." As if to indicate his agreement with his wife's views, Mr. Bentley said, "Discipline's what they need alright. . . . they don't realize it now, but they'll see it later. This discipline of cadets will run into later life." [7]
>
> MOTHER AND FATHER, SEPTEMBER 1969

The Egalitarian Creed

Parental concern with discipline is tied up with a number of related attitudes, not the least important of which is an allegiance to "The Egalitarian Creed." [8] Frequently sidestepping the realities of the situation,

[7] Ausubel's observations lend support to the suggestion that discipline appeared to be a subject of prime concern to parents regardless of their position in life: "No aspect of New Zealand life, with all of its many paradoxes, was more puzzling to me than the inordinate and reverential emphasis placed on discipline in the home and at school. In talking with parents and teachers the problem of discipline came up so recurrently that I was unmistakably left with the impression that in their eyes discipline and training were practically synonymous, and that the most important aim of both child rearing and education was to train the child in unquestioning obedience and deference to adult authority." David Ausubel, *The Fern and the Tiki,* pp. 84–85.

[8] Ausubel notes: "The New Zealander's belief in egalitarianism is obviously one of the major themes in his national self-image and character structure. . . . Doctrinally, from the standpoint of the New Zealander, all people, irrespective of their

New Zealanders appear to take special pride in the oft-heard claim that "No one in this country is better than anyone else. And that includes the Prime Minister." As if to underscore that boast, the telephone number of the Prime Minister is listed in the telephone book. Anyone so inclined is always free to put in a personal call.

"The more equalitarian a society the more likely that people will feel they ought to ignore differences of social class in their interpersonal relations, even though they actually perceive the subtle symbolic evidences of such differences." [9]

The field notes catch something of this egalitarian concern, together with certain egalitarian inconsistencies:

> As Mr. Baldwin's earlier response to my question about why he chose Boys' High for his son wasn't particularly telling, I pressed him further. This time he raised a subject of special concern to most parents—that of egalitarianism—an alleged belief, characteristic, or both, of New Zealand society to which most Kiwis I have encountered cling dearly— all the more in the face of the obvious fact that their society, for all its intentions, is not as egalitarian as they might like to think.[10] But, in clinging to this cherished ideal, the point nonetheless has to be made

station in life, are intrinsically valuable and important. . . . No one is inherently any better than anyone else. . . . According to prevailing doctrine, as soon as a millionaire or minister of the Crown leaves his office, no indication of his occupational importance should be visible in his social behavior. . . . If he walked into the bar for a beer, he'd 'act just like one of the boys and you'd never be able to pick him out.' " *Ibid.,* pp. 27–28.

Mitchell states: ". . . New Zealand is an egalitarian community with a myth of classlessness. . . . Classes do not obligingly differentiate themselves by nuances of accent, attitude or dress, nor can they be immediately distinguished in terms of a highly segregated educational system. Nevertheless most people do appear to be able to differentiate themselves socially by their vote and to accept the traditional class labels of working or middle class. . . . Only 11 percent in Christchurch . . . declined to put themselves into these class categories." Austin Mitchell, *Politics and People in New Zealand,* p. 211.

[9] Bernard Barber, *Social Stratification* (New York: Harcourt, Brace and Co., 1957), p. 217.

[10] There is considerable difference in New Zealand between egalitarian ideals and egalitarian realities. Ausubel draws attention to this distinction: "Ideological egalitarianism as manifested in popular belief, legislation, and political doctrine is not quite the same thing as egalitarianism in everyday personal relationships . . . it is immediately apparent from the observable kinds of interaction that occur in offices, shops and factories that hierarchical distinctions and deferential attitudes are much more explicit than in the United States. The casual observer at morning tea, for example, is left in doubt less frequently about who is headmaster and who is teacher, who is employer and who is employee, who is professor and who is student, and who is junior and who is senior in the departmental hierarchy. University degrees and academic titles are brandished quite ostentatiously; and titles of nobility are taken far more seriously in practice than one would anticipate from people who profess to scorn the British attitude in such matters." David Ausubel, *op. cit.,* pp. 30–31.

from time to time—Mr. Baldwin being no exception—that "We're all equal," even though, in point of fact, some equals are more equal than others: "The Old Man went there you know," he explained laughingly out of reference to his old boy status. "I don't want you to think I'm uppish," he continued quite on his own. "I'm no better than anyone else . . . I'm just a postman . . . but Boys' High has always had a standing. To say you've come from Boys' High means something. It's not a rag-bag school is what I mean to say . . . it can mean a decent job. The kind of people who come out of there usually wind up with jobs like lawyers, dentists, M.D.'s, and so on." "And are these considered the better jobs?" I asked. "Yes," he answered, hesitating just a little. "Then some people, in fact, are going to be better than others, despite all this talk about no one being any better than the next fellow, right?" I stated. "Okay. Yeah," he acknowledged halfheartedly. "And you're sending your boy to Boys' High because at heart you want him to be something better, isn't that also right?" I pressed. "Wouldn't you want the best for your children?" he offered.

EXCERPT FROM FIELD NOTES, OCTOBER 1969

The concern with equality readily translates into a less frequently acknowledged obsession with uniformity. It expresses itself in many ways, but most notably, perhaps, in the desire to see schoolchildren at least looking equal by having them looking identical. Nothing quite so nicely serves this felt need than the greatest leveler of social differences of them all, the school uniform:

"Uniforms are an excellent idea . . . easier to cope with . . . makes everyone look alike," she noted. "What's so important about them looking alike?" I queried. "Keeps people on the same level. Some people might not be able to afford clothes—could develop an inferiority complex," she explained.

MOTHER, OCTOBER 1969

The step from uniformity to conformity is easily managed:

Mr. Wright at first spoke of the uniform simply as effecting discipline for the better: "I feel when they're all in one uniform, discipline can be made easier," he stated. "In what respect?" I inquired. "Boys can go along as a common team—somewhat like an army unit. One goes along because everyone goes along. Makes them more amenable to discipline. Otherwise you might find you encourage them to fight the system." It was Mrs. Wright's turn to pick up the conversation: "Perhaps what we're saying is we should regiment them—mold them now— there's time for self-expression at varsity (university) later. Once they've formed in this common mold they can get around with other things later on." Mr. Wright wasn't exactly ecstatic over his wife's emphasis on molding and regimentation—not necessarily because this might not be an accurate accounting of things, but rather because the sound of such talk went "against the grain." "We don't like to say conformity," he stated by way of qualifying his wife's remarks, "but as I said earlier, we have to conform throughout our lives, from the day we're born." [11]

MOTHER AND FATHER, OCTOBER 1969

While parents were in agreement regarding the need for instilling discipline in the young, they varied considerably according to socio-economic standing and extent of formal education concerning the manner in which this was to be accomplished. The point is brought up at the quarter mark of the interview schedule:

> If anything is emerging that can be called a pattern among the parents I have so far interviewed, it is that they are sympathetic to the problems of the young in proportion to the extent of their own formal schooling and relative position on the socio-economic ladder. The lower one's position in these terms, the more inclined is one to adopt the simplistic view that harsher, more authoritarian measures are all that are necessary to instill in the young a strong sense of responsibility and self-discipline. The higher one's position, the greater the inclination to appreciate the problem in its fuller significance, the more likely is one to express the view that for the young to exert themselves in even semi-responsible fashion, they must be given in return the opportunity to engage in at least semi-responsible practices.
>
> EXCERPT FROM FIELD NOTES, OCTOBER 1969

Of the 20 sets of parents interviewed, approximately one-half expressed sentiments toward the youth that could be categorized as "sympathetic to understanding," whereas the remainder held attitudes ranging from "less than sympathetic to completely lacking in understanding." The one item that both groups held in common, however, was "the boy's best interests."

Typical of the attitudes of the first group were these comments: "We try to reason things out with our kids," "Boys 14 or 15 are old enough to know the true values in life," and "The kids of today are a sight better than we were." The following statement is paradigmatic of the perspectives toward the young of the "sympathetic to understanding" group:

> By and large, they're not a bad lot. We see and hear more about the noisy ones. But there are probably hundreds of responsible kids we never hear about at all. We've got to some extent to hand over more seniority to them. We've somehow got to take them more seriously.
>
> FATHER, OCTOBER 1969

[11] Oliver observes of the New Zealand character: "Security and equality are national obsessions. They take precedence over individuality and liberty. . . . The very pressures towards egalitarianism and conformity are strong enough to run to extremes." W. H. Oliver, *The Story of New Zealand* (London: Faber and Faber, 1960), p. 278.

Parents falling into the second category expressed the following views: "Young people don't know what's good for them; they have to be told," "You can't talk to Kiwi boys—caning's the only thing they understand," and "Boys will always say they haven't enough freedom to think." Typical of the attitude toward the young of the "less than sympathetic to completely lacking in understanding" group is the following:

> "Hair's another thing," he exclaimed. "I mean long hair . . . it's not just to force discipline on them. I mean proper discipline. . . . I feel that the masters at that school are trying to be too friendly with the boys, too familiar. Familiarity breeds contempt—too much psychology." "Are you saying there is a need for even more discipline at the school?" I asked, trying not to sound too incredulous. "I am," he stated loudly and clearly. Recalling the days when he was a boy there, he noted that "In those days monitors were a real force around there . . . they had the power to cane a boy." I then referred to the recent newspaper article suggesting that corporal punishment in the schools be abolished. "Would you like to see caning abolished?" I asked. "No," he answered firmly. "Definitely no. It ought to be retained—tightened up. If anything, more discipline is needed."
>
> FATHER, OCTOBER 1969

The Manliness Theme

A final but relevant prelude to parental perspectives on caning has to do with "The Manliness Theme." As an expression of adult concern with the passage from boyhood to manhood, it stands as a crucial link between disciplinary practices at Boys' High School and disciplinary expectations of the larger community.

The following excerpt is a continuation of the conversation with the same Mr. and Mrs. Martin referred to in an earlier section of the chapter ("Why Boys' High?") and is typical of most parents' concern with "manliness." The passage also serves further to illustrate the manner in which hypotheses emerged, were entertained in relation to the study's problem, and were either confirmed or rendered doubtful throughout the working course of the research:

> I finally told Mr. Martin that it struck me as rather strange that he placed so much emphasis on his son's becoming a man, and that he had referred to this at least five or six times in the course of the last half-hour's discussion. "How come?" I asked. He looked at me, slightly bewildered, then said, "Don't you want your son to be a man?" "Sure," I replied, "but I don't have to make such a point of it as you do. Besides, I'm not sure I even understand what you mean when you talk of being a man." He thought a while on that one. "I sort of mean—a good job in life—a better life—a respectable citizen of the community."

This is a point I shall have to further pursue in subsequent interviews. For I am fairly convinced that even if being a man implies responsible membership in the adult community, it means something more than that in New Zealand society generally. Being a man still smacks of toughness in the purely physical sense of the word—a point which makes a lot of sense in view of boys' inclinations to put on a visible show of toughness when taking their canings.

Mrs. Martin jumped in at this point. As though she had been reading my thoughts, she emphasized the connection between discipline and manliness, and just as important to her, the importance of having their son attain manhood: "I think discipline makes more of a man—someone who will handle himself in a responsible way." I next asked both parents if they were saying that being a man meant, in part, being a well-disciplined individual. They agreed that this was what they had in mind. "What about the discipline at Boys' High?" I asked. "Do you feel it is possibly too strict, not strict enough, or what?" "No," Mrs. Martin replied, "it's just nice. Helps to make a man of him. I'm all for discipline—especially for boys."

OCTOBER 1969

The meaning of manhood on the adult view can be seen to operate at two levels. On the first—as indicated by the comments of the Martins—manhood is equated with strong, wholesome character and with mature, responsible, self-disciplined participation in the life of the community.[12] On another, less sophisticated, less publicly acknowledged level, manhood is identified with toughness in the largely masculine sense of the term. This latter aspect of the social meaning of manhood is aptly demonstrated by still another passage in the continuingly informative discussion with Mr. and Mrs. Martin:

Since both parents seemed to equate manhood, in part, with self-discipline, I brought up my observation about boys at the school behaving in a manner that resembled anything *but* self-discipline: "When the master is in the room, the boys are fine," I stated. "But the minute he leaves, they raise holy hell. This doesn't strike me as behavior of the self-disciplined variety." Mr. Martin's response, boiled down to its essen-

---

[12] In a 1954 survey of parental expectations of the schools, Havighurst noted the importance which the New Zealand parent attached to the development of moral character in the young: ". . . . the principal preference is for the schools to contribute to the moral character of boys and girls. This is followed at some distance by education for citizenship and education to develop the reasoning powers. Fourth on the list is the traditional function of the schools—to teach reading, writing, and arithmetic. Then comes education for socio-economic mobility or a better position in life, and at the bottom of the list is the function of helping the boy or girl get into the university." Robert J. Havighurst, "What Parents Expect of the Schools," in Havighurst's *Studies of Children and Society in New Zealand* (Christchurch, New Zealand: Canterbury University College, Department of Education, 1954), Section VII, p. 4.

101

tial inconsistency, was that you're not a man if you're not self-disciplined, but if you behave in too self-disciplined a manner, you're not a man: "You see, one or two boys usually start the noise," he explained, doubtless speaking from experience. "Then the rest start in. If you don't join in, you're chicken, gutless. You're not being a man."

OCTOBER 1969

As something of a corollary to their concern with "being a man," parents expressed the view that manliness is best attained by the restriction of one's contacts at the crucial 13- to 16-year-old period to other males. Hence, in part, the preference for a boys' school:

Mr. Peters at this point pointed to the advantage of Boys' High from still another standpoint—the by-now-familiar concern with manliness. There were times when he made Mrs. Peters wince at his diatribe about the "natural superiority" of men over women: "I feel Boys' High has got much more to offer boys . . . they can give boys much more understanding . . . boys as boys, boys as men. It's unnatural anyway for boys 14 or 15 to chase girls. Seventeen or 18 years old, that's different. But at 14 or 15 it's much better for boys to be their own way." "I'm not quite sure I understand what you mean by that," I asked. He went on in his more than self-assured way. "A boy feels from, say, 13 or 14 that he's a little superior to girls. He wants to look down on them. If he's in a co-ed school he's brought down to their level. At Boys' High he feels he's a man." "What do you mean when you say, 'He feels he's a man?'" I pressed. He had a great deal of difficulty, for the first time, in explaining what he did mean, but he tried. It was clear that his last comment constituted the bedrock of his philosophy—that stage at which one no longer questions the basis of one's beliefs for fear, perhaps, of watching them fall to pieces. One simply "knows," without really knowing at all: "A boy has got to feel he can achieve something—that he can take his place alongside other men. I don't mean physical he-man stuff—that he's got to be with sports or that. I mean a buildup of behavior, of his character."

FATHER, NOVEMBER 1969

Perspectives on Caning

In light of the preceding statements, it is no surprise that the 40 parents interviewed voiced approval of caning at Boys' High by the overwhelming margin of 35 to 5. Of the 5 disapprovers, 4 were mothers. Several points stand out.

First, corporal punishment no more is an issue of pressing concern among parents than it is among boys and masters. As with the latter two sets of participants, caning is so entrenched a part of the system that parents seldom raised the subject of their own accord. As one reticent mother put it:

102

its boys if this image is to be upheld. The Headmaster made the point emphatically at this morning's assembly: "Since our return from the holidays it has come to my attention that two rules of this school are not being obeyed—those having to do with the proper length of hair, and caps. I'm surprised quite honestly that some of your parents would even have allowed you to return to school with your hair looking this way . . . you're letting this place down. I'm not asking that you have your hair in a short cut. We simply want to see it neat and tidy and well-groomed. . . . I'm just a bit fed up with having to track down people to see that they do something they should know enough to do on their own. . . . I've seen boys in the school and on the streets with unkempt hair and without caps where people know you're from this school. You're letting this place down. If anyone does not see fit to obey these rules it will take only a phone call to your parents, and arrangements can be made for you to go somewhere else. From now on I've asked monitors to report these things to me. . . . I'll see the boys concerned. If you're alright, that's fine, we'll let you go. If it's the second time, I'll cane you. I will not have you letting this school down."

SEPTEMBER 1969

The concern with the school's image is by no means confined to the Headmaster. Masters feel similarly:

If I see our boys on the street, I like to think they're making a good impression because they're from this school. I don't like them to be what I think Boys' High should not be.

SEPTEMBER 1969

Predictably, the subject of the school image is viewed considerably differently by the boys themselves:

I asked the boys exactly what seemed to be the staff's objection to the length of some of their haircuts. "That's what we'd like to know," one answered. Another offered, "Probably just the need to conform . . . they're afraid that if they let us grow our hair as we see fit, there will be five or ten boys who will grow it so long that people will see them and say, 'Look at those boys. They're from Boys' High. How awful.' The trouble is, letting our hair grow is the one way we have of expressing our individuality. Look at our suits—conformists gray. But you just can't injure the reputation of this place." "Well," I jokingly suggested, "You could all wear brush cuts." "Don't laugh," one jumped in, "two years ago one of the boys shaved all the hair off his head, walked into school, and said 'Is this short enough?' Well, they wouldn't let him back in for three weeks—until he started growing his hair back."

SIXTH FORM BOYS, APRIL 1969

Clearly it is not so much a concern with the individual boy that is at stake in these situations as an obligation to the inviolability of the

111

school's image. To a considerable extent in this regard, Boys' High is a victim of its past. For its present image is a carefully sculptured, even more carefully preserved product nearly one century in the making. It is not only that the Headmaster, masters, and even many of the boys feel an obligation to one another and to the school to maintain this sacred image. In addition, they feel constrained by the expectations of anyone and everyone—real or imagined—throughout the whole of Christchurch. The main worry is that these "others"—namely the public and the parents—will identify long hair and slovenly appearance with the school. The identification, of course, stands to harm the school's traditional reputation. In all of this, as the preceding excerpt makes abundantly clear, boys are expected to carry their share of the load. They are constantly reminded that this is not just any school. Rather, this is *the* school. One does not simply attend Boys' High. In a very real sense, one belongs to it.

The 3A3 Incident

Nothing better illustrates the part played by the cane in the molding process than "the 3A3 incident."[2] It occurred toward the end of the school year, at a time when Third Formers, as one master put it, "are finding their feet":

> It was a typical Friday afternoon at Nancy's Pub. "Here's something for your thesis, Joe," Jack Frobisher said, turning to me with a twinkle in his eye.[3] As Jack explained it, he and the other four masters who teach 3A3 had decided that, as a class, 3A3 had become too precocious for its own good. Something had to be done. All five masters agreed that on Wednesday each of them would insure that at least one member— one scapegoat from 3A3—got caned in every class that day, to drive the point home that it had gone as far as it was going to go. In Jack's own words: "Well, Bill had no difficulty pulling a boy out. It was the first class of the day. But then the little rascals caught on." "You mean you figure they knew what you all were up to," I asked, "that you were after their scalps to teach them a lesson?" "Oh, sure they knew . . . so by the

[2] 3A3 refers to the third ranked academic stream in the Third Form. The Third Form is composed of seven such academic streams—3A1, 3A2, 3A3, 3B1, 3B2, 3C1, and 3C2.

[3] This comment may indicate to the reader that at least some of the masters were "on to" my specific interest in corporal punishment. In fact, this was not so. Rather it is an indication that: (1) caning is a socially significant item of interest among the masters themselves, and (2) masters sensed my interest in matters of social control, but only as one aspect of my larger concern with the policies and practices of the school generally. I purposely queried masters at the conclusion of the study to determine if any of them had suspected my specific interest in caning. They indicated quite honestly that they had not.

next class they weren't about to make a move. But old Jim—he just waited. Then a boy turned around to borrow a pen from another boy, and Jim took 'em both out in the corridor. He gave the boy who borrowed the pen three, and the other boy two for lending it. The next class was Dave Fisher's—you can always count on him for a couple. He kept the chain going. But I've got to hand it to Don, here," he nodded in Don's direction, surrendering the floor for the moment. Don then explained how he finally found a way to keep the chain going despite the boys' attempts to break it: "They didn't make a move. I couldn't get them to say 'boo.' So finally I said to Mills—who hadn't said anything—'What was that you said, Mills?' 'Nothing,' he answered. 'What did you say, Mills?' I asked him again. 'Nothing,' he said again. 'I'll teach you not to add a "Sir" on to that when you're talking to me,' I told him, and I took him out and gave him two." (Laughter all the way around.) Jack now regained the floor to admit that, "By the time they got to me I couldn't get them on a thing. I really felt awful, 'cause that meant I was the weak link in the chain. But I finally got one the next morning, so I felt better." "And you were just trying to teach them a lesson—these boys are pretty good, actually?" I questioned. "Oh, yes, yes . . . they're a good bunch of boys—smart," he stated. "But they were just letting their class go down. I lectured them the day before. . . . I warned them, 'You're letting your class degenerate.' But it didn't do any good. You could talk yourself blue in the face to them. They just needed a good caning. Since then they've been fine. It's the only thing that could have settled them down."

OCTOBER 1969

The rationale for the "plot" to shape up 3A3, as well as an indication of the amount of organizational effort behind it, is acknowledged by the Master-in-charge of Third Form boys:

"Just what did 3A3 do to bring the wrath of the masters down upon their little heads?" I inquired. Laughingly, he explained: "About this time of year Third Formers are getting used to the place . . . they're feeling their legs for the first time. They literally go mad. And they'll keep on going mad until about the middle of their Fourth Form next year when they start to settle down again. Meanwhile they're trying things out, as a way of testing their legs. But 3A3 went completely over the bloody edge. Fortunately I have a good group of willing masters who were ready to cooperate as a team."

OCTOBER 1969

The Masters' Caning Book—exhibiting a flurry of officially recorded entries unprecedented for a mere two-day period—lists the "offenses" and corresponding punishments meted out to various chosen representatives of 3A3:

10/9	Norton	3A3	Homework ignored	(2)
10/9	Mills	3A3	Homework incomplete	(1)
10/9	Mills	3A3	Work incomplete and stupid behavior	(2)
10/9	Cook	3A3	Talking after warning	(3)
10/9	Waring	3A3	Provocative talk after warning	(3)

10/9	Vance	3A3	Talk after warning	(2)
10/10	Cook	3A3	General stupidity	(1)
10/10	Norton	3A3	Imposition not done	(1)
10/10	Mills	3A3	Lack of manners	(2)
10/10	McKay	3A3	Lack of manners	(1)

FROM THE CANING BOOK, OCTOBER 1969 [4]

In answer to the question, "Did it work?" one turns to the estimations, however subjective, of those on either end of the means to the end:

I raised the subject of the 3A3 episode with one of the masters involved, noting that I had heard bits and pieces about the incident from some of the others. He laughed good-naturedly. "How is 3A3 getting on?" I asked. "Very, very well indeed," he announced. "Now only the scintillation of an eyebrow is sufficient to cause them to desist from any unnecessary talk." "Just what was their problem?" I asked. "Well," he explained, "it was only five or six good rebels—highly intelligent boys, very intelligent indeed—intelligent enough in fact to devise some rather shrewd schemes for disorder. Intelligence, you know, correlates highly with idleness. You use your brain not to work but to get others to do your work for you. Anyway, it was only these five or six intelligent, spirited rebels. But the rest of the class was beginning to follow them. I could see something was going to have to be done because they would come to me from the class before—this woman's class—and it was obvious they'd been having the time of their lives. This woman teacher was unused to handling this sort of thing and they had her on the edge of a nervous breakdown." "And I suppose, being no dummies, they knew what was about to befall them," I suggested. "Oh, absolutely," he replied. "They'd had their fun, and they knew they would have to pay the price." "But now you feel they're coming around," I offered. "Oh, yes. The improvement is remarkable . . . and I would say their work has improved 60 percent. The other day one of the boys had enough courage to come up to me and say, 'Why can't you treat the rest of us as kindly and nice as you used to? You treat us like animals and you bark at us all like dogs when it's only five or six who are making the trouble. The rest of us have been doing our job.' I said to him, 'Listen, young pup. I was addressing my last remarks not to those five or six rebels, but to the personage of you. You were the one who saw fit to turn around to talk to your neighbor just a moment ago.' He knew he was wrong, of course, at that point. He hung his head low and agreed. I said, 'But thanks anyway, Warwick, for being the guinea pig.' And he saw the point of it all." In a final, telling reference to those five or six "good rebels," he noted, "Frankly, I like this kind of boy—full of spirit—in fact, I must say they remind me of myself in my day. You know," he concluded, "you have to recall your own experiences as a boy to be able to deal with these lads."

OCTOBER 1969

[4] In Chapter 4 it was estimated that the average number of caning incidents at the school were five per day. The figures on which this is based were accumulated over a five-month period prior to the occurrence of the 3A3 incident. In other words, the offenses cited in connection with the 3A3 incident were not used in the estimation made in Chapter 4.

As for the boys themselves, perhaps the following is as informative an answer as one will get to the question, "Did it work?":

Mr. and Mrs. Clark had heard a good deal about 3A3's recent run-in with their masters through their son, Jamie, one of the members of that ill-fated class. When asked about the incident, Mr. Clark replied laughingly, but with an unmistakable air of approval: "Yep. 3A3. Naughtiest class in school." As they had heard it from their boy, only a handful of upstarts had precipitated the reprisal. Jamie—who by now had been called in to speak on his own behalf—noted that, "A few chaps were making it difficult for the rest of the class to learn." "And is the class shaping up?" I asked him. "It sure is," he announced certainly. "Mr. McKenzie doesn't even bring his cane to class anymore."
INTERVIEW WITH PARENTS, OCTOBER 1969

In fairness to the masters involved, it should be noted that "the 3A3 incident" was not characterized by animosity, or ill will:

"The 3A3 incident" was not conducted in an atmosphere of sadistic reprisal but of reasonable humor and good will. Because boys—especially "better" boys such as those of 3A3—indicate by their behavior that they do not always know what is best for themselves, because they are inclined to have the system on, because they are bent on a bit more spirited rebelliousness than is commensurate with the school's hallowed image, and not least, because these boys—coming from an upper academic ability stream—represent the potential cream of the school's crop, one has to appreciate from the point of view of the masters that it is in boys' own best interests that they be dealt with firmly in these kinds of situations. In the case of 3A3, something had to be done and it was. The rebellion was quelled—with considerable success from all accounts. The boys, having undergone their "baptism under fire," were welcomed back into the fold in the fashion of the prodigal son. The system has been challenged, the uprising as usual has been put down, the Boys' High image remains intact, the boys once more know what is expected of them, the cane has served its purpose in the molding process, life goes on.
EXCERPT FROM FIELD NOTES, OCTOBER 1969

"The 3A3 incident" may be further understood in terms of the system's special need to mold its so-called "better" boys. If anyone is in need of being duly processed, it is those boys who constitute potentially the leaders of the community. It is therefore of the utmost importance that they, in particular, be ingrained with an appreciation of what is expected of them as early in their young careers as possible. Furthermore, if one takes the view that society's leaders traditionally have been those who pay obeisance to its norms, and if one accepts as well the suggestion that Boys' High is in the business of training society's leaders—or at least that it sees itself as doing such, a self-appraisal supported by facts such as that in 1960 the Chiefs of Staff of the New Zealand Army, Navy, and Air Force all were old boys of this school—then the importance of molding young potentates along acceptable lines becomes understandable, and the significance of the cane as an instrument in the molding process all the more understandable.

Molding as exemplified by the caning of Third Formers is but a specific instance of a general situation, however. While the cane may indeed have its greatest effect as an instrument of socialization at the Third Form level, it is a useful adjunct in the molding of Fourth, Fifth, and occasionally Sixth Form boys. It functions to keep boys in line, to shock them into submission by making an immediate impression on them, to discourage notable differences among them—all with a view to the standardization of a product fulfilling the highest expectations of the school and all that it stands for. As the keynote speaker at the annual Old Boys' Reunion noted, "It must be our job to instill what we take to be the essence of this school in every boy." Nevertheless, the cane need not be applicable in all situations, nor for that matter, to all boys. Some submit willingly and are therefore not in need of physical coercion; others are smart enough to conform, if only superficially, in the interests of expediency. But for those neither willing nor smart enough to fall into line, there is always the cane standing by as an effective reminder—refreshing one's awareness of who he is, namely a boy of *this* school, while at the same time reinforcing an 88-year-old image of what one is on the verge of becoming, namely an old boy of a very special establishment. What the school uniform is to uniformity of appearance, the cane is to uniformity of thought and attitude.

The Bonding Process: Boy to Master to School

Still another function of the cane has to do with the part it plays in "the bonding process." This term refers to the cane's potential for effecting bonds of personal devotion, unquestioning loyalty and obedience, camaraderie and *esprit de corps* among boys, masters, and school. The bonding process thus deals in part with "that old school tie," in part with the interpersonal relationships of the participants.

One becomes aware of the existence of the bonding process through incidents and statements such as the following:

> "Caning is a personal relationship. A boy places himself in the position of a son to his father. . . . by bending over, a boy shows he can stand up to his punishment and take it. It's tribal. Of course it is. We haven't yet rid ourselves of the tribal in us you know." Continuing in this vein, he related a story that further confirms my suspicions concerning the

that he was a pretty good bloke." He went on to note that the cane needn't affect every boy as it had affected him. It depended on many things: "That's why you have to be so careful," he stated earnestly. "You can't just use the cane on anyone—indiscriminately. Some boys will get caned and hold it against a master all through school; others will be buddy-buddy right after."

Sixth Form boy, August 1969

Granted the bonding potential of the cane, there remains the problem of specifying the kinds of boys, the type of master involved, and whether the bond is one of mutual obligation or one-sided attachment. The following is a consideration of that problem:

Mutual Bonding—Boy to Master to Boy: As one reflects upon the phenomenon of the bonding process—and especially upon the personalities involved—it is clear that the master in a mutual bonding situation is the kind of person who is a bit more insightful, a bit more thoughtful, and above all, considerably more sensitive of his role in relation to boys. Despite their typically blustering, tough, even physically foreboding "front," they are genuinely concerned with what they like to call "the boys' best interests." For all their hazing and loud reminders (Socks up," "No talking," "Hands out of your pockets," "Caps on"), they take their responsibilities seriously—more seriously than the "average" master. They see themselves as *in loco parentis*. This deep-felt responsibility is a prime ingredient in the kind of "mix" with respect to which the cane may be said to have *mutually* bonded boy and master.

Mutual bonding is further characterized by both parties' acceptance of the cane as an appropriate response to the offense in question. Both boy and master, in other words, must view the misdemeanor as one deserving of the cane. In view of the widespread acceptance of the CIE/CIA perspective, this usually is a matter of course.

Finally, boy and master alike must have a sense of the significance of the occasion. That is, they must sense that the caning is no laughing matter, but rather that it signifies "the signing of a contract," the beginning of a new understanding. Otherwise, as in so many cases where respect for the seriousness and attendant significance of the occasion is lacking, the entire episode is "nothing but a big joke," in which case, it may be just as remembered by a boy, it may be just as lasting in its impression on him, but it will not have had the effect of bonding him, morally, to the will of the master.

One-Sided Attachment—Boy or Master: What of bonding in its one-sided sense, be it with respect to boy or master? If the one-sidedness of the bond applies to the master, then the forementioned ingredients of a sense of responsibility and sensitivity, and a belief in the justice of the

119

punishment, still apply. What is missing for the transformation to be a mutual one is either an appropriate corresponding sense of responsibility and sensitivity on the boy's part, or the acknowledgment that the punishment is, indeed, a fitting one. Where the one-sidedness of the bond applies to the boy, on the other hand, it is fair to say that *he* now views the situation with sensitivity and a new-found feeling of responsibility, whereas it probably can be said of the master that the whole affair served only as an outlet for his pent-up frustrations, the more quickly forgotten the better. The following excerpt illustrates the point:

> Warren is master-in-charge of the camera club. This, he suggests, is one of the few situations in which he comes to know the boys "on a friendly, even first name basis." "The boys open up quite a bit at these club meetings," he noted. "They talk to me. It's remarkable how they remember their canings. Someone will come up to me and tell me about the time I caned them. And they're absolutely surprised when I tell them I don't even remember it—I've forgotten all about it. They think you're going to hold a grudge against them forever—like every time you see him after you've caned him, you're going to say, 'I hate his guts.' Well, you don't do that at all. There's no malice intended. I tell a boy after he's been caned, we wipe the slate clean. That's that."
>
> While Warren senses boys' reminders of their canings as an indication of resentment, I see the episode as an indication of their personal attachment to him, given the cane as the cement that "glued" or bonded the two together. Their reminders, I suspect, are intended to bring to Warren's attention that they once experienced something in common—the boy's submission, Warren's subjection, and not least, the attendant, all-encompassing emotional release that lent to their momentary encounter a certain aura of crisis, shared involvement, and mutual personal attachment. Furthermore, the incident illustrates the one-sidedness of the bonded relationship. That is to say, where the caning incident signified something of a lasting personal attachment for the boy—given his recollection of it to Warren, coupled with his surprise at Warren's absence of recollection—the incident apparently had no such lasting effects, no such signification of personal attachment to Warren—inasmuch as he claims to have completely forgotten the incident, if not the particular boy as well. In short, what Warren's comments suggest is that whereas caning may bond boy to master, it need not, conversely, bond master to boy. In most cases, the bonding effect of the cane probably works mainly to the advantage of the boy.
>
> EXCERPT FROM FIELD NOTES, JULY 1969

The Kind of Boy: What of the *kind* of boy who is inclined to be subject to the effects of the bonding transformation? Typically, he is a Third or Fourth Former, for the reason that these are the "youngsters," so to speak. These are the lads most immediately in need of being molded to the staff/community-sponsored image of a Boys' High boy. They're new, and they don't yet "know the score." They're probably not even terribly certain anymore of who they are, but they know they're on the verge of being something different than what they have been up to this point. Being so new, but being also so full of life, they are in the position of having to be brought as rapidly as possible into conformity with "the party line." And that usually means an encounter with the cane, directly or otherwise.

Bonding in its mutual sense involves the kind of boy for whom a caning is a grievous matter, a situation requiring of him a sense of personal obligation to the administering master in the fullest, or near-full moral sense. This is the more serious boy—the academically minded lad who has "slipped up," but who, realizing his mistake, does not intend to let it happen again, to let misbehavior or insurgence stand in the way of his real purpose for being at Boys' High, namely, learning and academic achievement. That, then, is the one kind of boy—the kind who takes his work and his objectives seriously, and equally important, who has the intellectual capacity to meet Boys' High on its own battleground, that of academics, if not sports.

The less than academic types are more likely to bond—or better yet, attach themselves to masters—in highly one-sided fashion. Lumping these types together, we can say that their personal attachment to a master is one-sided and exclusive because it lacks the ingredient of responsible, moral obligation, without which there cannot be a "signing" of a contract.

Still another type is the sporting lad, the physically aggressive boy— not at all an incomprehensible sort of fellow given the school's emphasis on sporting excellence. The sporting lad revels at the prospect of physical contact, be it nothing more than the friendly jostling that characterizes boys' movements up and down the corridors during the morning and afternoon breaks (or even in class), or the more intensive jostling witnessed on the playing fields. Being a physically active person, he is less visibly submissive than most. For him the cane, which probably only temporarily puts him in his place, is but an extension of his thriving for physical exchange.

The bonding process thus can be seen to be highly complex in character, depending as it does on the temperaments of the participants, as well as the nature of the situation. Given the "proper mix," however, it is clear that the cane can and does function as a bonding agent. The phenomenon reflects the inherent impersonality of the system—and particularly the reservedness of the boy-master relationship—and may be seen as an adjustive response of the participants in meeting that situation.

More than merely serving to bond boys to masters, the cane bonds boys to the school. Old boys' fond recollections of their canings—even to the point of romanticizing their experiences—illustrate the point:

> "Caning's pretty rare nowadays," he noted none too certainly. "Not that way in my day. I can remember when class was in high glee because one old master—Jeffcoat—would chalk his cane, leaving a white mark on the seat of a boy's pant. Then he would chalk it again, and everyone would wait to see if he could hit the same mark twice in a row. And the boy who got it was a hero. Mind you, not anyone who got caned was a hero—not if you were caned for getting caught drinking at the Waimate Pub or something. But the interesting things . . . the ceremony of it."
>
> OLD BOY, SEPTEMBER 1969

And another recollection:

> Recalling his days as a boy of the school, he spoke of an old master who "was so highly respected and liked by all the boys that it was the ambition of every one of them to be caned by him." "I don't quite understand," I responded. "Well," he explained, "old Dave—this master—was a lovely bloke. It was good to have a caning or two from him. He used to have an alarm clock in his room—to keep track of the time. Boys weren't supposed to enter the room before he arrived. But they did of course. And they would set the alarm to ring halfway through the period. Dave would say, 'Alright. Which boy did it?' And, of course, the boy would own up to it willingly. Then Dave would have him come to the front of the room for his caning."
>
> OLD BOY, AUGUST 1969

Certainly these anecdotes paint a colorful picture of the brighter side of caning. But in addition to that, they illustrate the ritualistic, even tribal character of the phenomenon. They suggest that caning be seen as something of a ceremony, a rite of passage, an almost mystical bond that ties boys to one another, to their masters, and to the school, and moreover, that it does these things in ways which an outsider would be hard-pressed to appreciate.

Being Good at Being Bad

Still another function of the cane has to do with the so-called "hard-core belt notcher" discussed in Chapter 5 ("Jim"). That discussion centered around the escalatory tendencies of belt notching, the changed significance of the ritual in proportion to the number of notches displayed, the resulting decline in peer-group standing, and finally, the recognition by others that the hard-core belt notcher has a problem.

Having failed to make their mark via the accepted routes of academic or sporting achievement, boys like Jim typically resort to one of the few routes left. If they can't be good at anything else, they can at least be good at being bad. The hard-core belt notcher thus finds himself repeatedly misbehaving chiefly as a means of gaining attention. Caning in these instances functions as a substitute for recognition and human affection. For whatever else one may wish to say about the cane, the one thing that boys like Jim can point out is that at least there is *someone* on the other end of it. The tragedy is that boys such as these go on misbehaving, while the teacher goes on punishing, neither understanding what is really happening. Some of the more astute participants recognize the situation for what it is:

> They say the more marks you get on your belt, the more guts you're supposed to have, the tougher you are. But I don't think that's it at all. The bloke who gets the most canings is the boy who isn't very good at anything else. This is his way of being good at something. It's sort of a symbol for him. If he can't be good at other things, he figures he can at least be good at this, even if this means being good at being bad.
>
> FIFTH FORM BOY, JULY 1969

The need to engage in this kind of status seeking is traceable in large measure to the character and organizational makeup of the school itself. It is an indication of the pressures on boys to excel. It is the result of an unrelenting atmosphere of competition. It has equally strong roots in the impersonality and reservedness of a large, foreboding institution. The youngest, most impressionable, and usually most awed boys are confronted in rapid succession with a series of requirements that force them either to find themselves in a hurry, to establish an identity compatible with the makeup of this particular establishment, in short, to be someone, or in the end simply to be lost in the shuffle.

From the standpoint of the system, the acknowledged deviant behavior of boys like Jim effectively enforces the norms of the school. For to the extent that others view Jim's conduct as irregular, they regard their own behavior as normal—that is, as in keeping with the system's expectations.

Punishment and the Cane

Masters' remarks to the effect that, "When I do use the cane, I use it well . . . so that the word gets around," illustrate a further function of the cane, one which stands in support of Durkheim's suggestion that punishment serves not so much to admonish the individual offender as to reinforce in the minds of others the inviolability of a given rule.

. . . the essential function of punishment is not to make the guilty expiate his crime through suffering or to intimidate possible imitators through threats, but to buttress those consciences which violations of a rule can and must disturb in their faith—even though they themselves aren't aware of it. . . . For what gives the rule its authority is the child's view of it as inviolable; any act that violates it promotes the belief that it is not in fact inviolable. . . . If the teacher permits a lapse in this respect without intervening, such leniency bears witness—or seems to, which amounts to the same thing—that he no longer deems it so worthy of respect.[5]

The following two passages clearly indicate masters' awareness of this point:

David noted that, because he goes home for lunch, unlike most masters, he is more apt than the rest of the staff to see boys "without caps on." He finds the situation personally awkward. "Well," he explained, "this is difficult for me. I see them, and they know I see them. And I look at my watch, and say to myself, 'I don't want to stop and be late again for lunch.' But because I don't stop and do something about it, they think I condone this sort of thing . . . and this is in front of all the other boys . . . whereas I suppose I should get out and cane them so the others will be reminded there's a rule about the wearing of caps."

MASTER, JULY 1969

"You mentioned caning boys only for serious offenses," I remarked. "I'm not sure I know what you mean by that." "Gross impertinence," he declared. "It's bad enough just in front of me. But when it's in front of the whole class—that's when it's really bad."

MASTER, MAY 1969

Both the above incidents allude to the recognition among masters that while offenses such as failure to wear caps and impertinence toward one's superiors are bad enough in themselves, what really is of concern is the inviolability of a given rule. The rules at stake here are that boys (1) shall be properly in uniform, and (2) will show masters proper respect. The punishment for disobediance of either of these rules functions essentially to renew and invigorate these understandings, since were they violated with impunity, the rules which express them, as rules, would cease to exist. In Durkheim's words:

The law that has been violated must somehow bear witness that despite appearances it remains always itself, that it has lost none of its force or authority despite the act that repudiated it. . . . Punishment is nothing but this meaningful demonstration.[6]

[5] Emile Durkheim, *Moral Education,* edited by Everett Wilson (New York: The Free Press of Glencoe, 1961), pp. 167, 175.
[6] *Ibid.,* p. 166.

"Caning Builds Men": A Last Look at the Manliness Theme

. . . although some adults look back on their secondary school days with a bitterness and resentment that has still not abated, many others tend to romanticize the entire experience and perceive in retrospect the beatings they received, deserved or otherwise, as marks of distinction. Besides serving as necessary instruments of retribution, canings were valuable and meritorious in their own right; they made men out of boys. A tanned hide was something to be proud of. . . . One couldn't be sure that one was really a man until one's backside had absorbed without the slightest show of flinching, the full fury of a master's wrath.[7]

It was suggested in Chapters 5 and 8 that the social meaning of manliness is significantly related to the perspectives on corporal punishment created by the participants. This section examines further the nature of that relationship.

The meaning of manhood at the adult level in its "sophisticated" sense —i.e., being a responsible, self-disciplined member of the community— takes the form of an attitude toward the young. Responding as best they can under the circumstances, boys frequently translate elders' expectations of manhood in its sophisticated sense into expectations of manhood in its unsophisticated sense—i.e., the overt display of masculinity: hence, in part, the belt-notching rituals and statements like, "It shows you've got guts if you can take it." By the same token, insofar as the adult definition of manhood is decidedly ambiguous, the adjustive response of the boys to elders' attitudes toward them is not entirely a result of mistranslation.

Of significance is the linking—via the social definition of manliness— of disciplinary practices at Boys' High with the disciplinary expectations of the larger community. That is, to fully understand the social meaning of corporal punishment is to take into account the social significance of manliness, the more masculine manifestations of which, one suspects, are rooted in the rough-and-tumble days of frontier New Zealand, a time when the male need for a show of physical prowess was a lot more real than it is today:[8]

[7] David Ausubel, *The Fern and the Tiki: An American View of New Zealand National Character, Social Attitudes, and Race Relations* (New York: Holt, Rinehart & Winston, Inc., 1965), p. 95.

[8] McGee speaks of myth and reality in the life of the ordinary New Zealander: "All societies create their myths. . . . New Zealand's myth is that it is a raw, pioneer, rural society. In reality, it is increasingly a mature urban society. Today most New Zealanders are urbanites; more correctly, suburbanites. . . . Glover's 'Arawata Bill' and Crump's 'Good Keen Man' are of the myth, gone down the brown, dirt-dusted, fern-sided roads with Lee's 'swaggies,' never to return. Now these bearded rogues with beery breath play their roles in the escapist dreams of the suburbanites, who subconsciously cherish the myth, but live the reality." T. G. McGee, "The Social

It's a man's, man's, man's man's world—so much so that it evidences itself at almost every turn one takes in one's social dealings—from the oft-expressed insinuation of the Rugby enthusiast that, "You don't mess with the 'All-Blacks' (they're real men)," [9] to boys' tendency to "take your caning like a man," to the phrase inscribed on the walls of one of its boys' schools, "Manliness Is True Virtue." The only question one might raise in connection with this last motto is whether it would not have been more in keeping with the Kiwi temperament had its subject and predicate been reversed.

EXCERPT FROM FIELD NOTES, OCTOBER 1969

Played to the accompaniment of "the manliness theme," even the tendency of boys to "push" masters takes on added significance. For pushing functions not only to ascertain masters' varying tolerance levels, but to discover, affirm, and reaffirm in the eyes of one's peers one's claim to manliness. This is accomplished either by bettering one's superiors in a test of wills, or by taking one's caning "like a man" in the event one oversteps the bounds of discretion. On either outcome, the boy is the winner. He has established his claim to manhood no matter what the result. [10]

The adjustive response of the boys to elders' expectations of manliness

---

Ecology of New Zealand Cities," in *Social Process in New Zealand,* edited by John Forster (Auckland, New Zealand: Lonpman Paul Ltd., 1969), p. 144.

Discussing the immense popularity among New Zealanders of Barry Crump's *A Good Keen Man* (Wellington, 1960), Cameron notes: "The phenomenal success of this piece of fiction is undoubtedly due to the fact that a culture hero has been born. Perceptibly true to life, the lone deer culler is shrewdly self-reliant in the bush, mock-heroically scornful and ill at ease in the life of the towns, cynically and almost boorishly detached in all but one or two of his personal relationships, adept at keeping the welfare state (which pays him) at arm's length, disarmingly enthusiastic about the minutiae of his work, impatient and scornful of inexperience and incompetence, sardonically tolerant of other men's idiosyncrasies, and, above all, intolerant of any form of social or civilized life. He is in fact a projection of the New Zealander's dissatisfaction with the comfortable mediocrity and stultifying conformity he has created in his modern welfare state, a modern version of the myth of the indomitable pioneering spirit of earlier generations." William J. Cameron, *New Zealand* (Englewood Cliffs, N.J.: Prentice-Hall, Inc., 1965), pp. 52–53.

[9] The "All-Blacks" (so-called because of their all-black dress) is the New Zealand national Rugby team. It rates consistently among the top amateur Rugby teams in the world.

[10] The intensely masculine tone of Boys' High bears out Murdoch's observation of nearly 30 years ago: "In some boys' schools, the 'he-man' tradition is very strong. . . . Referring to a proposal before his Board of Governors to abolish punishment by cane by the two head prefects one outstanding headmaster recently wrote: 'I ask the board whether they want me to add to the current deluge of sloppy sentimentality by turning out at _____ jellyfish and molluscs, or he-men with backbone and spirit tough enough to face the stern realities of life'." J. H. Murdoch, *The High Schools of New Zealand, a Critical Survey* (Christchurch, New Zealand: Whitcombe and Tombs Ltd., New Zealand Council for Educational Research, Series No. 19, 1943), p. 215.

varies, of course, as boys progress upward through the forms. That is, useful as is the concept that taking one's caning stoically is tantamount to an expression of manliness, it does not characterize boys generally. It has a genuine application in the Third and Fourth, increasingly less in the Fifth Form, and almost none whatever in the Sixth Form.

This situation reflects three things—first, the changed attitudes and expectations of others toward boys as they approach the world of adulthood; second, boys' changed definitions of manliness consistent with these altered attitudes and expectations; and third, the boys' growing maturity. In the Third Form one is awed by the system and all it represents, including the socially constructed view that Boys' High is the final steppingstone to manhood and that a means of indicating one's claim to manhood is by showing he has the "guts" to take his caning without so much as a whimper. Fourth Formers see the matter in roughly this fashion, though their views are on the verge of modifying themselves given others' expectations that they "behave like Fourth Formers now." If one does something "stupid," naturally one can expect to be caned, and there is still a need to "take it like a man." But the Fourth Form definition of manliness begins to take on a different meaning—that of disciplining oneself. The cane declines correspondingly as a significance of manliness. One is neither quite so proud, nor quite so boastful as before. By Fifth Form, "others" expect more still of a boy—"others" being the staff and that intangible but influential perspective of the boys themselves that "You grow out of caning by the Fifth Form." Caning thus further declines as a signification of manliness by the Fifth Form. Boys' attitudes at this stage range from unconcern to outright criticism of caning—not as something to be abolished, of course, but rather as a childish, immature activity to engage in, one that anyone with something so serious on his mind as School Certificate and pending University Entrance Examinations simply has not the time to be bothered with. By the Sixth Form, one's definition of manliness has altered still further. Caning no longer implies manliness any more than manliness has as one of its meanings, caning. This is a time when, except for blatant breaches of the rules, to be caned is an injustice, an unforgivable indignity. The caning of Sixth Form boys stands as a repudiation of the system's *raison d'être*. It violates everything that the school stands for. It is no wonder, then, to hear Sixth Formers referring to the cane as ". . . ineffective, immature, and childish." They are beyond it, though enough of them have insinuated that the cane "probably isn't a bad thing to have around as a last resort," that is, for the younger lads, the Third, Fourth, and possibly even Fifth Formers.

So caning signifies manliness, and manliness caning. But it is testimony to its ever-shifting stature—given the altered situational imperatives of the Third, Fourth, Fifth, and Sixth Form years—that the social meaning of corporal punishment does not stand still relative to moving, and above all, maturing participants in a changing social context.

Conclusion

Like the chapter preceding it, Chapter 9 has attempted to get at the basis of the social meaning of corporal punishment at Boys' High School. It has done this by examining some of the functions of the cane in relation both to the institutional character of the school and to various of the larger community's ideas, demands, and expectations. It has suggested that these functions may be seen largely as an adjustive response of the participants to the constraints of their school and community.

The purposes served by the cane as discussed in this and preceding chapters are by no means exhaustive. Rather they are a collection of what impressed this observer as relevant and sociologically interesting instances of the cane's many uses.

Chapter 10

A Valid Theoretical Context

I guess you just think like everyone else without ever asking why.
PARENT, OCTOBER 1969

The CIE/CIA Perspective Revisited

The study's central objective was to discover and explain the perspectives on corporal punishment of the boys, masters, and parents of Christchurch Boys' High School. A major perspective of the participants emerged in the form of the CIE/CIA perspective, *caning is expected/ caning is accepted.* The chief characteristics of the perspective are self-descriptive. Caning is an *expected* response to certain kinds of behavior in certain situations. The participants "know" under what circumstances they can expect caning. But, moreover, caning is an *accepted,* fitting response to certain kinds of behavior. It is sanctioned by the participants as a legitimate instrument of discipline. With few exceptions, the participants simultaneously expect and accept the cane. The two aspects of the perspective work in tandem.

The CIE/CIA perspective is one of the "facts" of school life. The actions and statements of the participants indicate that this is so. Indeed, their behavior is what gives this fact its existence. This is not to suggest the perspective is present to the participants all the time, or that it is the only possible way for them to deal with the school's requirements of them, or finally, that it is such a major concern so as to overshadow all others; caning, after all, is a significant, but not a salient feature of the school. Rather it is to say that Boys' High is organized so as to pose particular problems for the participants. Some of these problems involve the activity of caning. As the participants have handled these problems, they have developed collectively ways of dealing with and thinking about them that are reasonable and workable. That is, their perspectives are so constructed as to enable them to act with reasonable success in a problematic world. One such perspective created by the participants is that caning is an expected and accepted activity of the system. The CIE/

129

CIA perspective is one means, among many, of dealing with the problems of school life.

"Using" the CIE/CIA Perspective

The preceding section has implied that the actions and statements of the participants indicate in part that they "use" the CIE/CIA perspective as a means of coping with some of the problems of school life. Strictly speaking, however, the participants do not "use" this perspective, that is, they do not say to themselves, "I am now behaving so as to indicate to others that I expect and accept caning as a legitimate practice of this school." Rather, their ideas and actions in relation to caning are constitutive *of* the CIE/CIA perspective and indicate its existence. The participant does not consciously act out his part for the benefit of others any more than a person who is frightened acts with the intent of indicating to others his fright. The frightened person *is* frightened. His actions so indicate. Likewise, the participant in caning situations *is* expectant and acceptive of the cane. His ideas and actions so indicate. He is not acting. He is therefore not "using" the perspective in the sense that an actor would use it. Rather he is behaving in a way which indicates that the perspective is part of the natural order of his social environment and that he has acclimated himself to it. Nothing better illustrates the difference between the conscious use of the perspective by the actor on stage as against its unconscious use by the participants in live situations, as the following:

> I thanked "my" five Third Form boys for letting me spend the school day with them. I then went my way. They elected to remain in the vacated classroom for the five remaining minutes to the end of the period. They had found a three-foot length of scrap wood about the size of a cane sitting in the corner of the room. As I peered back at them through the window—to their obvious delight—I could see them acting out the various parts of caner and caned—bending over, taking a proper stance, practicing their swing, mimicking schoolboys and schoolmasters in a way that would have done justice to an amateur theatrical group.
>
> Excerpts from field notes, July 1969

Here the participants were using the CIE/CIA perspective as would an actor. Their actions still may be regarded as evidence of the perspective's existence. But they must also be seen as an instance of play-acting, as *consciously* intended to elicit a particular response from their audience —myself—and from one another.

The participant in actual caning situations does not act as in the preceding fashion. He knows that the live caning situation is real. To say that he uses the CIE/CIA perspective is to say that he thinks and behaves in ways which—though usually not consciously intended—indicate that the perspective is a natural part of his social order and that he regards it as something which "everyone knows." It is to say that he anticipates a certain regularity of response to his own actions from the other members of the school community.

The fact that everyone "knows" the perspective is both an indication and a consequence of the individual's capacity to assume others' attitudes toward him, as well as toward others, and to fashion his own behavior accordingly. The CIE/CIA perspective is an emergent of the participants' mutually adjustive responses to one another's attitudes and expectations in relation to the constraints of their particular environment.

Just as it is possible to speak intelligibly of the CIE/CIA perspective, it is possible to speak of "the CIE/CIA person." Within the Meadian framework, "the CIE/CIA person" is that aspect of the total personality of the individual which emerges out of the process in which the participants' anticipations of one another's responses are centered around the activity of caning. The adjustive responses to the system of first-year masters are prime illustrations of this point (see Chapter 7). The result in the form of a Larry Buller indicates that the process works. Indeed, Larry Buller is the epitome both of the process and the consequences of that process. He is proof that the CIE/CIA person exists, and moreover, that he is alive and well at Christchurch Boys' High School. The practice, the CIE/CIA perspective, and the CIE/CIA person exist only insofar as the participants see that the actions which others expect of them involve both the expectation of caning in certain situations and its acceptance as fitting punishment. The participants thus invigorate and perpetuate the CIE/CIA perspective through their behavior, while at the same time incorporating the perspective because it is a means of behaving consistently and acceptably with the behavior of the group.

Evidence for the Existence of the CIE/CIA Perspective

My own awareness of the CIE/CIA perspective was *not* the result of a conscious count of incidents and statements on behalf of its existence any more than the participants' awareness of it is the result of a conscious effort at incorporating it. Rather, various actions and statements of the participants—in conjunction with the style, manner, and emotional and psychological context of their presentation—combined with my own interactions with the participants so as to leave me with an understanding and appreciation of the perspective's significance. In short, I came to

TABLE 11

Items of Evidence for the CIE/CIA Perspective

		Volunteered	Directed	Total
Staff:	*Statements*			
	Alone	41	49	90
	Group	3	1	4
	Activities			
	Alone	5	—	5
	Group	16	—	16
	Total	65	50	115
Boys:	*Statements*			
	Alone	2	1	3
	Group	22	24	46
	Activities			
	Alone	—	—	—
	Group	1	—	1
	Total	25	25	50
Parents:	*Statements*	5	27	32
Total items of evidence for participant use of CIE/CIA perspective		95	102	197

"know" the perspective because it is something that everyone at the school "knows."

Evidence of the perspective's existence is discoverable in items from the field notes—discussions with boys, masters, and parents, statements overheard, descriptions of incidents, and so forth—which take one or more of the forms described in past chapters. Any item having one or more of the characteristics of the perspective as it has been described is taken as evidence of its existence. And conversely, the existence of the perspective is born out by its capacity to interpret and give meaning to items from the field notes. The number of such items is presented in Table 11. While the study acknowledges the existence of participant sub-perspectives on corporal punishment—i.e., "Caning is a nice thing to have around," "Caning is cathartic," the "Caning as a last resort" syndrome, and so forth—these are treated, for the most part, as derivatives of the CIE/CIA perspective, and are counted as evidence of its existence. The field notes yielded a total of 115 items indicating staff use of the perspective, 50 items on behalf of its use by boys, and 32 items for parental use, or a total of 197 pieces of evidence indicating participant use of the CIE/CIA perspective.[1] It is unlikely that a perspective which is either insignificant or nonexistent would appear so frequently in the field notes.

Admittedly the subject of caning frequently was interjected into the interaction by the observer. However, the nature of the interjection usually was sufficiently unstructured—i.e., "What are some of your feelings about caning?"—as to permit the respondent to express himself freely. The participant was thus encouraged to discuss those aspects of caning which came to him "naturally." The evidence also suggests that use of the perspective is frequent and widespread, and furthermore, that it is collective in nature, shared for the most part by the participants and not developed by each of them independently.

One has to evaluate this conclusion in another way, however. The number of items from the field notes reflects the number of hours spent in the field. One might obtain sufficient items of evidence to support almost any claim about a school if he waited long enough. I was involved with the study daily for nine months. I interacted regularly and freely with the participants in all kinds of situations during this time. Evidence for the CIE/CIA perspective likewise presented itself on numerous occasions and in varied circumstances both in and out of school.

Negative items—i.e., those indicating that the participants do not accept or failed to act in accordance with the perspective—are infrequent and insignificant when measured against the number of items in support of the major perspective.[2] The field notes yield only 25 negative items (staff—9, pupils—9, parents—7), 12 percent of the total number of items considered (206). This indicates the absence of competing perspectives among the majority of participants. Furthermore, the negative instances cited do not specifically indicate a rejection of the CIE/CIA perspective. Rather they suggest that some of the participants view caning as ineffective, immature, and unnecessary, or that they do not consider caning an appropriate expedient under all circumstances but, by the same token, that they consider it a "good thing" for the system as a whole, or finally, that they are able to operate within the system on a different set of premises. In other words, the negative instances documented in the field notes do not cast doubt on the existence and widespread acceptance of the perspective itself.

Ultimately the reader must interpret these figures for himself, keeping in mind the character of items from the field notes. On my own view, it is unreasonable to maintain that the perspective was either insignificant

[1] A sample of items of evidence for the CIE/CIA perspective appears in the methodological appendix.
[2] A sample of negative items appears in the methodological appendix.

or infrequently used by the participants, or that it was the creation of my imagination.

Use of the perspective was extensive. Items from the field notes were gleaned from a variety of informants—boys of varying ages and academic abilities, boys with different interests, boys who were coping successfully with the system and those who were not; masters young and old, masters returned as old boys of the school, masters from elsewhere, masters with little or no teaching experience, "old-timers" with records of 20 and 30 years' service; parents of boys across all forms and streams, parents of varying socio-economic backgrounds and degrees of education. In other words, the perspective cannot be said to be limited to one group of individuals or type of situation.

Equally important, the perspective was collectively shared by the participants not only as something that everyone "knows," but furthermore as something that everyone knows "works." Proof that the perspective was collective in nature was especially evident among the boys: the collection of evidence from them—with few exceptions—involved interacting with groups ranging in size from 4 or 5 boys to classes of 15 to 30. But the perspective was evidently collective in character with respect to masters and parents as well. The overall consistency of their actions and statements supports this claim. Were the perspective not held collectively by them, this observer would not have been able to make use of the terms contained in it without provoking argument, disagreement, or expressions of incredulity. Nor would the field notes be replete with instances in which the tenets of the perspective served without question as a basis for group action.

The fact that the perspective is used without difficulty or disagreement shows that it is so commonly held as to be accepted unquestioningly by the participants as something that any "reasonable" person would know and understand:

> These people in the papers—the ones who want to get rid of corporal punishment—ought to go have their heads seen into. They don't know a thing. Someone ought to put them in front of a class. Then they'd see.
> MASTER, MAY 1969

Social Meanings, Adjustive Responses, and Others' Exceptations

Although the CIE/CIA perspective is shared collectively by the participants as something that everyone "knows," various derivatives of the perspective—i.e., "the caning as a last resort" syndrome, belt notching as significant of manhood, and so forth—are not shared by all the participants as much as they are part of the symbolic repertoire of particular

134

groups. That is, granted the existence of the CIE/CIA perspective as one of the prime facts of school life, different groups—and groups within groups—incorporate the perspective in response to differing situational imperatives. Common acceptance of the perspective does not at the same time guarantee commonality of the meaning of caning on all fronts, nor among moving and maturing participants in changing situations. The meaning of caning to a Third Form boy—i.e., signification of manhood and/or group belonging—differs sharply from its meaning to a Fifth or Sixth Form boy—i.e., an injustice and/or denial of maturity—and even more sharply from its meaning to a master or parent—i.e., "It means I've lost control," or "He won't push me that far next time."

The discovery of differences of meaning among the participants is consistent with the study's symbolic interactionist premise, which has suggested that the meanings of things are a complex function of the desires—individual and collective—of the participants, the demands and expectations of others in the system, and the various situational constraints in relation to which individuals adjust to one another and to their environment. To alter the variables in the mix invariably is to modify the social meanings which emerge from them. Thus one would be surprised *not* to discover variations of meaning among different groups responding to considerably different demands and exceptions—even within the framework of the same system. The following incident illustrates the point:

> I don't like caning. . . . I don't use it. It's animal-like isn't it? If I did, the boys would be absolutely shocked—and I'd lose rapport with them for a week, it would set them back so. I prefer not to cane. It doesn't achieve anything. It doesn't put the burden of responsibility on the boys' shoulders. I try to give them a reason for everything I do. . . . Now, as hostel manager, I cane. I feel the situation there is different, more domestic. I tell the boys I'm like their father—and caning is the ultimate punishment.
>
> MASTER, JUNE 1969

Clearly this indicates that the perspectives on corporal punishment of the participants are different in part because the participants themselves possess the capacity to assume the attitudes of others toward them and to adjust their own behavior accordingly. At the same time, the hostel manager's rejection of the CIE/CIA perspective in the one situation where it has been shown to exert its greatest influence—i.e., the school—illustrates still another point. Granted the overwhelming influence of the perspectives of the group, there is always the possibility, indeed the likelihood, that at least one individual member of that group will reflect the given pattern differently. In this way the entire system of meanings, however minutely, also is affected and changed. For just as the one individual reflects the universe of meanings in a way that is unique to himself, his own reflection is picked up and reflected by others. In Mead's words:

> . . . the organized structure of every individual self within the human social process of experience and behavior reflects and is constituted by the organized relational pattern of that process as a whole; but each individual self structure reflects and is constituted by a different aspect or perspective of this relational pattern, because each reflects this relational pattern from its own unique standpoint, so that the common social origin and constitution of individual selves and their structure does not preclude wide individual differences. . . .[3]

Mead further suggests that "the logical structure of meaning is to be found in the threefold relationship of gesture to adjustive response and to the resultant of the given social act. Response on the part of the second organism to the gesture of the first is the interpretation and brings out the meaning of that gesture." [4] The following incident supports this claim:

> Not all masters keep cane in hand for use on a moment's notice. Therefore it is not unusual to have a boy knock on the staff room door with the request, "Mr. Smith wants to borrow a cane." The boys appearing at the door to borrow the cane, of course, usually are the very ones upon whose backside it is about to descend.
>
> I followed the boy who came to borrow a cane this morning and witnessed—at a distance—his punishment. A Sixth Former, he received four of Mark Hopkin's best. As Mark later explained it to me, "He and another boy were tearing each other apart in class." While the boy admitted as much to me on his way back to return the borrowed cane, he explained in his own behalf that, "Sure, I was joking around with this other bloke, but I didn't think he'd stand up right in class."
>
> As seemingly insignificant as this encounter might have been, it enforced my notions about (1) the emergence of several distinct meanings with regard to the same incident dependent upon social context, and (2) the process via which these meanings come into being. I note the contrast between the boy's embarrassment and tight-lipped manner when confronted with my question, "What happened?" as against his laughing, joking encounter with two of his friends over his caning only moments later. I do not know precisely what was the meaning of his caning to that boy within the context of his encounter with me. But I strongly suspect that whatever was its meaning to him then differed considerably from its meaning to him at the time of his laughing, joking encounter with his friends. And if his caning held different meanings in

---

[3] George Herbert Mead, *Mind, Self, and Society,* edited by Charles W. Morris (Chicago: University of Chicago Press, 1934), p. 201.

[4] *Ibid.,* p. 80.

these separate situations, this is reasonably explained in terms of the contrasting social contexts in which the boy found himself, particularly in that the boy's response in my presence differed from his response in the presence of his friends. It would not have been "appropriate" for him to laugh and joke with me, for example—that is, unless he felt it safe to presume that my response to his laughing and joking would have been to laugh and joke in return. Anticipating anything *but* this kind of reaction, he responded otherwise; for the most part he hardly reacted at all—an indication probably of his uncertainty of my likely response to his own. In fact, the boy was at a complete loss for a response until I finally brought our encounter to an end with the remark, "Well, at least it's over and done with," to which he, for the first time, let go a smile of relief and—departing—said, "Yes."

JUNE 1969

This passage indicates once again that the basis of meaning is to be found in social conduct—that is, that the meanings of things are a result of the capacity of individuals to assume one another's attitudes and expectations, to anticipate the resulting responses, and finally, to adjust their own behavior accordingly. Additionally, however, it suggests that the responses of individuals which are constitutive of the meanings of things are responses to the thing itself in only a secondary sense. Indeed, they ought not to be thought of as responses to some thing or event at all. Rather, individuals' responses are to others—specifically, others' attitudes toward themselves and toward others. The meanings of things are social in character for having emerged in relation to and as a result of social exchanges in socially created situations.

Negatively, this says something about what a social meaning is not. It is not so much an idea in someone's mind about a given event—or about the meaning of that event—as it is an adjustive response to the likely or anticipated-as-likely response of others to one's own adjustive response. As one's responses become less adjustive and more automatic —because one comes to "know" what is expected of him—the response comes to be taken for granted. It is conditioned. The point, however, is that it is not conditioned as a result of one's reaction directly to some object-stimulus or event. Rather it is conditioned as a consequence of one's anticipation of other's expectations, these expectations eventually being taken for granted as something that any reasonable person would expect. Thus individuals unquestioningly and unconsciously filter out— or let in—the meaning of a given object-stimulus in terms of their responses to others' expectations. The object-stimulus may be despised, loved, harmful, sacred, unspoken, scandalous, or amusing; it may even be unseen. Sensory stimuli, in other words, are selectively filtered. The filters, however, are social in character. Ultimately they take the form

137

of vocabularies which, in the process of naming, both indicate some object-stimulus and supply the normative response to it. It is primarily in terms of these kinds of socialized responses, these group perspectives, that we can state what people, individually and collectively, take to be the meanings of things.

So it is with the perspectives on corporal punishment created by the boys, masters, and parents associated with Boys' High School. In their origins, these perspectives may be seen as an adjustive response to the anticipated responses of others in the system. It is at this stage that one witnesses the emergence of the perspectives on caning of the participants. It is only later—given the repetition of these responses to repetitious events, given the pre-existence of a group perspective—that one's responses become less adjustive and increasingly automatic. It is then that the social meaning of corporal punishment takes hold of the individual to the point where the perspectives on corporal punishment of the group are accepted as his own. Much like the proverbial fly caught up in the spider's web, he succumbs to the network of meanings that has been spun for him by generations of others. Individuals "cave in" to the particularistic moral demands of their social environment because, in fact, they have no choice. As one first-year master in the process of adjusting to the system put it, "I didn't want to cane. But it's part of the system. If you're going to take teaching at this school seriously, then you're going to have to conform. And that includes the cane." The willingness of the individual to live, work, play, and in general, to get along with others in social situations which he deems important to his livelihood and well-being is an *emergent* of his interactions with others, not something which he brings with him.

Other Persons, One's Self, and Institutions

Mead draws a useful distinction between the self and the human organism. The self is "that which has a development; it is not initially there at birth but arises in the process of social activity." [5] It is distinct from the person seen as physiological organism proper.

The process out of which there emerge social meanings is the same process responsible for the development of the self. The creation of the self, like the creation of the meanings of things, has it basis in social conduct. Selves develop as a result of the capacity of the individual to step outside of himself, to see himself as an object much as others see him. He does this indirectly, by assuming the particular standpoints of others in the same social group, or the generalized standpoint of the

[5] *Ibid.*, p. 135.

social group as a whole to which he belongs—what Mead calls "the generalized other":

> The organized community or social group which gives to the individual his unity of self can be called "the generalized other." The attitude of the generalized other is the attitude of the whole community.[6]

Insofar as the individual is able to take the attitudes of others toward himself within the social environment or context of experience in which both he and they are involved, he becomes conscious of himself as an object or individual, and thus develops a self or personality. Others' attitudes toward the individual, in conjunction with the capacity of the individual to see himself from that standpoint and to adjust his behavior accordingly, give him a self-identity. In other words, one's self is the creation of individuals' mutually adjustive responses to one another's attitudes and expectations. One's self, one's particular identity, indeed one's existence as a human being as opposed to a human organism, is a consequence of the capacity to assume others' attitudes.

This is why it is possible to speak sensibly of "the CIE/CIA person." He is that aspect of the self which has emerged out of the process by which the attitudes of the generalized other result in the kinds of mutually adjustive responses among the participants which indicate that caning is an expected and accepted practice of the system. Insofar as these responses are incorporated into his behavior, it is possible to speak of him as "the CIE/CIA person." Indeed, it is no more unusual to speak of the CIE/CIA person for having incorporated into his self certain attitudes and responses with respect to the activity of caning, than it is to speak of the loving, the stern, the permissive, or the conservative person for having incorporated into his self attitudes and responses expressive of these characteristics.

There are within the school community—as has been shown—whole series of responses centered around caning which the participants hold in common. These responses—in conjunction with the attitudes in relation to which they arise—constitute the *institution* of corporal punishment at Boys' High School. This institution is composed of the common attitudes—and the attendant common responses—of the members of the school community toward a particular situation.

> . . . an institution is, after all, nothing but an organization of attitudes which we all carry in us, the organized attitudes of the others that control and determine conduct.[7]

[6] *Ibid.*, p. 154.
[7] *Ibid.*, p. 211.

The CIE/CIA person is the individual who, via the process of generalization, is able to assume the attitudes toward him, which center around caning, of the members of his whole community and to conduct himself accordingly. He responds to others' attitudes toward him because, in fact, he has no choice; that is, because responding to others' attitudes toward himself and fashioning his behavior accordingly is what it means to be a participating member of that community.

The extent to which the individual's response to a particular situation differs from that of the group generally, varies with the character both of the individual and of the community. That is, the same community that gives the individual a self, gives him a mind:

> Human society . . . does not merely stamp the pattern of its organized social behavior upon any one of its individual members, so that this pattern becomes likewise the pattern of the individual's self; it also, at the same time, gives him a mind, as the means or ability of consciously conversing with himself in terms of the social attitudes which constitute the structure of his self and which embody the pattern of human society's organized behavior as reflected in that structure. And his mind enables him in turn to stamp the pattern of his further developing self (further developing through his mental activity) upon the structure or organization of human society, and thus in a degree, to reconstruct and modify in terms of his self the general pattern of social or group behavior in terms of which his self was originally constituted.[8]

Usually we view the world as composed of other persons, one's self, and institutions. And we regard the institutions as being the result of persons and selves interacting. But on the Meadian perspective, *persons and selves* are the results of the interactions.

> . . . the contract theory of society assumes that the individuals are first all there as intelligent individuals, as selves, and that these individuals get together and form society. On this view societies have arisen like business corporations, by the deliberate coming-together of a group of investors, who elect their officers and constitute themselves a society. The individuals come first and the societies arise out of the mastery of certain individuals. . . . If, however, the position to which I have been referring is a correct one, if the individual reaches his self only through communication with others, only through the elaboration of social processes by means of significant communication, then the self could not antedate the social organism. The latter would have to be there first.[9]

That is why it is important to develop an understanding of human behavior not by looking at the institution, but rather by looking at the

[8] *Ibid.,* p. 263.
[9] *Ibid.,* p. 233.

ideas and actions of persons as a means of accounting for the character *of the institution*.

Conclusion

Corporal punishment at Boys' High holds different meanings for different people and/or groups of people. It is a signification of peer standing and group belong to some, an indication of the attainment of manhood to others, the "ultimate" deterrent or the "only conceivable" punishment to still others. It has the paradoxical potential for bonding individuals to one another, and to the school—seemingly forever—or for driving them apart—also, seemingly forever. It is a useful instrument of socialization, a means of belonging, a convenient administrative device, a tension-reliever *par excellence,* and many other things.

The group perspective that presides over all these meanings is that caning is both an expected and accepted activity of the system. Who expects and accepts caning? Everyone—or almost everyone—which, from the standpoint of the participants is to say that "others" expect and accept caning, and moreover, that they expect one to react in certain ways to it. The various responses which constitute the meanings of caning are thus collective in character, regarded by the participants as something that everyone—or at least everyone within particular groups—"knows." Ideas and actions which at first sight appear to be matters of individual judgment, motivation, and behavior, on closer inspection are seen to be collective in character, a reflection as well as a consequence of the group's ideas and actions. The significance of this point cannot be emphasized strongly enough. Irrespective of which side one takes in the debate on corporal punishment in the schools, it behooves him to appreciate the collective basis of the phenomenon if he expects to understand or deal effectively with it.

To recognize that the perspectives of the participants are *collective* in character is to recognize as well that they are *social* in origin. That is, the meanings of caning to boys, masters, and parents can be seen to inhere not in the phenomenon of caning as some essential aspect of it, but rather in the participants' mutually adjustive responses to one another's expectations in socially created situations.

Two factors lie at the heart of the social meaning of caning at Boys' High School—the overwhelming strength and influence of the CIE/CIA perspective, and the capacity of the participants to assume one another's attitudes and to mutually adjust their behavior accordingly. The statements and actions which constitute the meanings of corporal punishment have their basis in the capacity of the individual to respond in ways that are expected of him. Persons interact in social situations, they are subject to one another's "feedback," and they adjust their conduct on the basis of it. The group's meaning—allowing for the fact that each individual reflects the given universe of discourse uniquely—becomes their meaning. The perspectives of the community become their perspectives, and vice versa.

Finally, individuals' mutually adjustive responses to one another's expectations—besides constituting the meanings of things—give the person his personality and character, in terms of which he may be said to be a self, rather than merely a body. The process via which meanings are seen to be social in origin thus is the same process which transforms human organisms into human beings.

Postscript: Some Closing Thoughts

Courtesy

I can be courteous, you know.
  Road courtesy;
Because it makes the roads nicer to drive on. If everyone . . . . .
  Courtesy to people because I respect them.
  Courtesy to my parents;
  Courtesy to anyone I respect and like.
    (It comes naturally.)
  Courtesy to masters.
Even
  Courtesy to masters I don't respect or like.
That is,
I am polite; I try not to put a foot wrong,
Mainly because of habit,
  convention, and the rod.
Because might is right.

There are two sorts of courtesy.
Both exist.
Both have a reason for existing,
Though one is natural
  and one artificial.

But my crime was surely not
  Wilful discourtesy
(If I'd wanted to insult him
I'm sure I could have thought of a
Better way) (Now I do, and I can);
but Accidental discourtesy.

—Perhaps I ought to write
An essay
  on
Accidents.

A SIXTH FORM BOY'S PROTEST, JULY 1969 [1]

[1] As already has been noted, the First Assistant rarely canes Sixth Form boys. Rather, as "punishment" for their occasional indiscretions, he assigns essays appropriate to their offense. The author of the above was charged with discourtesy toward one of his masters and sent to the First Assistant. Told to write an essay on courtesy, he chose to present it in the form of a poem.

I have attempted throughout the preceding chapters to look at the activity of corporal punishment from the point of view of the participants, analyzing that phenomenon in the interests of making sense of it, but, insofar as possible, avoiding evaluations of the practice itself. Looking back on eleven months of intense involvement with the subject of corporal punishment—nine of which were spent interacting daily with the participants—I am confronted with the suspicion that I returned from my New Zealand experience with much information, but—not really to my surprise—correspondingly less wisdom. Be that as it may, one does not come away from so impressionable an experience without having made certain judgments. I pass them on because, much in the fashion of those masters who would not hesitate to give a boy a "hiding" in his own "best interests," I feel a deep responsibility to Boys' High for having granted me the privilege of being a part of it. But just as I am personally obligated to apprise the school of my assessments, I must in the same breath offer it a piece of advice attributed to William Makepiece Thackery—"As soon upon learning that someone is coming to my house for the purpose of doing me good, I beat a hasty retreat out the back door."

In Answer to Some Arguments

The arguments on behalf of caning at Boys' High take several forms. Most of these can be answered—after a fashion. But to the extent that the kind of arguments associated with corporal punishment rise more often from sentiment than reason, and equally important, given the exceedingly collective character of the perspectives on corporal punishment of the participants, one suspects that the net effect of any answers will do more to strengthen the convictions of opposing groups as to one another's ignorance and obstinacy of opinion than to settle the matter "once and for all."

The first such argument is that of the masters—"I use the cane only as a last resort." The evidence of the past chapters speaks to the contrary. Rather—and this is especially true of the younger, first-year master—caning is the first, not the last response. One dispenses with intermediary reprisals such as verbal reprimands or detentions largely out of recognition of their "inconvenience":

> "Some say caning is the ultimate weapon—you know, first written assignments, then detentions, then caning. I'm not so sure it works that way," he stated. He went on to suggest that it usually worked the other way. One first went for the cane, mainly because it was expected, but also because it was quick. He attested to the cane as a convenient,

"lazy" form of punishment with the remark, "Besides, you have to grade a detention." "And that takes time," I offered. "That's right," he agreed.

FIRST-YEAR MASTER, JULY 1969

The fact that the older, more experienced masters cane infrequently —and in some cases not at all—is not a claim in support of the "last resort" argument so much as it is an admission of the *needlessness* of the cane's employment.[2] As one "old-timer" put it:

> "I've got a cane in my closet, but I haven't taken it out in eight years. You know what I mean?" "That's pretty good," I acknowledged. "I can do better by getting at a boy with words," he continued. "But, to recapitulate, I wouldn't want to see it go. I would want to see it kept—as your last trump card."
>
> MAY 1969

Actually, one doesn't require years of experience to recognize the needlessness of the cane. One young master in his second year noted:

> I caned a lot last year. It didn't really do that much good. This year I've only caned a boy once. I did it because I was just fed up. And then I did what you should never do. I told the boy, "If you do that once more, you'll get caned." I committed myself. Then the next time I had to cane him. But I feel that if a teacher runs a really interesting class, he needn't resort to that.
>
> JUNE 1969

The rejoinder of the masters that "I cane only for the serious offense" is equally faulty—that is, unless one accepts a definition of such misbehavior as "talking in class," "running in corridor," "impertinence," "slamming door," or "singing in class" as serious.[3] If the cane *is* the ultimate deterrent at Boys' High, then it is ultimate in terms of what by most standards are minor, trivial—though admittedly disruptive—offenses. In other words, the school's definition of "serious offense" is applicable chiefly within the context of the school itself. The cane thus is not so much ultimate as convenient. One master who acknowledged the point put it this way:

> It's not the ultimate as a deterrent. It's simply the accepted punishment. If a boy steps out of line, he knows what to expect.
>
> JULY 1969

[2] The cane is not "needless" in the sense that it has no function within the school. The preceding chapters have built a powerful case for the fact that it serves a host of functions. Rather, the term "needless" means, given that some masters claim to get along as well or better by not employing it, the cane is not an indispensable instrument of discipline.

[3] See Table 6, *Caning Offenses at Boys' High School from 1925 to 1969.*

As for those offenses which *are* deserving of the title serious—i.e., cheating, lying, stealing, truancy, drinking—the effectiveness of the cane as a deterrent—much less as a genuine solution—is admittedly inappropriate:

> . . . but not for cheating or stealing—because there's something more at the bottom of that—caning won't do.
>
> MASTER, AUGUST 1969

A further argument has to do with participants' seeming inability—or rather, reluctance—seriously to entertain alternatives to corporal punishment. The "argument" usually is of the form, "What else have you got if you give up the cane?" Alternatives, in point of fact, are not unknown to masters. Rather, they are disclaimed. For, in actuality, one need look no further than the New Zealand school system itself in citing alternatives to corporal punishment. In sheer contrast to the disciplining of boys, for example, corporal punishment of secondary, though not primary schoolgirls is frowned upon, if not expressly forbidden. Granted, it is possible—as one so often is told—that "boys are another kettle of fish," that they are more obstreperous than girls, hence in need of the kind of punishment which leaves a physical stamp on their backsides in addition to a psychological imprint on their mentalities. But this view is barely arguable. Schoolgirls, not to belabor the point, are no less ingenious than boys in their capacity for mischief.

What, then, *does* one do with misbehaved young ladies? According to the Headmistress of one girls' school with whom I spoke, cantankerous females are, in order, verbally reprimanded, given detentions which range from written assignments to after-school chores, or sent to the Headmistress for a "talk." In serious cases, parents are invited to the school for a consultation. Ultimately a girl faces expulsion. The absence of corporal punishment in these situations, not to mention its abolition with apparently successful results elsewhere in New Zealand,[4] flies in the face of claims to the effect, "What else have you got?" Rather, these expressions of inconceivability are better understood as (1) a reluctance to part with a time-honored, time-tested, and not least, convenient tradition, (2) an acknowledgment of the strength of the demands and expectations inherent in the CIE/CIA perspective, and (3) further indication that caning serves purposes beyond the mere "discouragement of wilful and deliberate faults."

---

[4] Kaitaia College—A New Zealand sceondary school—abolished corporal punishment and noted a dramatic improvement in length of stay, attendance, and attainment of its pupils. Michael Sequin, "Research Facts About Corporal Punishment Which Many Ignore," *National Education* (New Zealand), June 3, 1969, p. 226.

Proponents of the cane are quick to note that the Kiwi boy is a different sort of lad, that "a good caning is the only thing he understands." And there is a certain truth to this claim. But if the Boys' High boy, if not the Kiwi lad generally, is indeed different, his difference may be reasonably seen to be the result of a thorough, though well-intentioned cultural indoctrination. To use the words of one of the few of the school's masters educated outside New Zealand:

> "These boys are pretty reasonable and sensible—basically good," Bill suggested. "If caning were dropped, they'd find themselves." "But, Bill," I detracted, "I have personally asked boys numerous times what would happen if caning were abolished at this school only to be told, 'We would go wild.'" "That's how bloody much they've been brainwashed, Joe," he shot back. "I think that in time they'd see they were ruining it for themselves."
>
> APRIL 1969

Because caning has been so completely socially indoctrinated in boys, they tend unquestioningly to accept it as part of the "natural order." Those who embark on a teaching career frequently are inclined to carry on routines familiar to them from their youth, thus reinvigorating the cane's institutionalized standing in a manner best described as self-perpetuating:

> Referring to a boyhood acquaintance now teaching at a private boys' school in the area, Ian noted: "Peter was strapped throughout the primers and caned at secondary school. When he became a prefect (monitor) he caned, I think, every chance he got. Now he's teaching, and I'm sure he uses it still. From the way he talks, I think he'd rather die than give up the cane."
>
> UNIVERSITY FACULTY MEMBER, JULY 1969

Caning Works

In fairness to corporal punishment's practitioners, it may be that the preceding criticisms, ultimately, do not matter. Perhaps caning *is,* in the words of the Headmaster, ". . . just another form of punishment." So long as it is not shown that corporal punishment is in any way detrimental to its objects, what does it matter that it is self-perpetuating; that it frequently is used as a first response rather than a last resort; that its effectiveness as a deterrent is at best questionable; or finally, that it serves purposes of an extra-disciplinary nature? The boys mostly appear to hold up well in caning situations. There is little resentment among them; they stand united in support of the cane's retention. In the sense that it is an accepted, unquestioned, institutionalized practice, caning "works."

To the extent that caning functions to the satisfaction of the overwhelming majority of the participants, one is inclined to echo one master's view, "Why all the fuss?" Indeed, were it not for one or two items, the disinterested observer might well be content to let the matter stand —to say, "If this is what everyone wants, why not?"

But there *are* difficulties with the system of corporal punishment at Boys' High, the failure of the school's participants to acknowledge the point notwithstanding.

First, as an extension and a reflection of an essentially authoritarian system of discipline, the practice of corporal punishment in the schools is inconsistent with the disciplinary practices and expectations of an adult world. As Ausubel suggests, this poses a problem:

> It is not that authoritarian methods of discipline, in and of themselves, are necessarily incompatible with the development of strong occupational drives and methodical work habits. In the course of growing up it is possible for children implicitly to accept conscientious attitudes toward work that adults inculcate in an authoritarian fashion. Evidence from contemporary Germany and Japan also indicates that young people are able to internalize such values, i.e., accept them as their own and acquire feelings of obligation to abide by them even when external controls are not applied. On the other hand, it is evident from the same evidence that the process of internalizing adult standards in an authoritarian setting only occurs if two other conditions also prevail. First, the culture must be consistently authoritarian at all age levels and in most face-to-face situations. Secondly, the standards in question must be generally observed by most people in the culture.
> Thus, older children and adolescents do not satisfactorily internalize values that are indoctrinized in an authoritarian manner if the adult culture itself is organized along democratic and egalitarian lines . . . not only do they tend to resent the authoritarian discipline that is imposed upon them, but also to conform to adult standards only under threat of external compulsion.[5]

Provided corporal punishment at Boys' High is not viewed as part and parcel of a boy's preparation for eventual admission into the adult world—which, of course, it is—the practice of caning is not inconsistent with the operation of the school itself. It fits in, and from all one can gather, works well at—and above all, within the confines of—Boys' High. But one is inclined to ask, "What about afterwards?" Has caning done anything to instill in boys the kind of self-discipline which, on the insistence of masters and parents alike, is so important to one's conduct

---

[5] David Ausubel, *The Fern and the Tiki: An American View of New Zealand National Character, Social Attitudes, and Race Relations* (New York: Holt, Rinehart & Winston, Inc., 1965), pp. 48–49.

in the outside world? Take the oft-heard implication that caning helps "make a man of a boy," allegedly by instilling in him a sense of self-disciplined obedience to the school's and ultimately to the larger community's rules. Actually, the instillation of self-discipline via the cane is doubtful. This point has evidenced itself repeatedly in this observer's observations of boys' "hell-raising" tendencies in the classroom in the absence, or even the presence of their masters. Moreover, corporal punishment is not used to maintain rules in the everyday world of New Zealand adult life. One does not get caned for showing late to work; one either is verbally reprimanded, or for failure to adjust accordingly, dismissed. Thus there is a hard and fast break between obedience to the rules at Boys' High under threat of physical punishment, and one's personal and societal obligations under possible threat of the loss of one's job.

The failure of masters and parents to recognize the inconsistency in their view of corporal punishment as socially legitimate preparation for self-disciplined participation in the adult world when measured against the disciplinary practices that actually operate at the adult level stem in part from the further failure to distinguish adequately between *self-discipline* and *externally imposed discipline*.

Self-discipline does not imply the right merely to do as one wants without concern either for its social consequences or for its effect on others. To be self-disciplined is to be free to respond to the expectations of other individuals, to be responsive to others, and in so doing, to be *responsible* to them. One's freedom, in short, has limits—namely, those moral obligations that derive from, and are an extension of others' attitudes and expectations toward oneself, much in the fashion—as a case in point—of the Headmaster of this school. The Headmaster, as he himself put it, is free "to run this school as I want to—completely." But that the Head's freedom is of a responsive, therefore responsible nature—that is to say, that the disciplinary restrictions imposed upon him are of a self-disciplined nature—is made clear by his own admission that, "If I take one step in the wrong direction, I know I'll have ten members of the Board of Governors to tell me so—politely, mind you—but they'll tell me." And the definition of a "wrong direction" is a composite of the Head's view and his anticipation of the Board of Governors' definition. But even without the Board, the Headmaster still would be responsible in a self-disciplined sense. For his responsiveness, hence his responsibility, is not merely to the Board of Governors; it is to boys, to parents, to masters, and ultimately to the community itself. For all his seeming autonomy, the Head's behavior reasonably may be viewed as an adjustive response to others' expectations of him. Within these bounds, however, he retains the right of a certain discretion and freedom of movement. The degree of freedom is externally imposed only to the extent that it involves the feelings and needs of the school and community; for the most part it is self-imposed in view of the Head's awareness and attendant response to others' demands and expectations.

In contrast to self-discipline, one can speak of an externally imposed discipline of an essentially nonmoral nature, that is, a form of discipline having as its prime mode of enforcement the threat of physical punishment. Self-discipline is distinguished from externally imposed discipline as follows. With respect to self-discipline, one's adjustive responses—and in the process one's responsibility—is toward equally responsive other individuals, or, in Meadian terms, the organized attitude of "the generalized other." With respect to an externally imposed form of discipline such as caning, the response is not so much to others' attitudes, as to the implied threat of physical punishment. The cane thus replaces those "others" and "others' expectations" as the object of response. But while one can morally respond to the expectations of others even in their absence—i.e., "Mr. Smith *expects* me to behave, so I will"—one cannot respond in similar fashion to a cane in the absence of its administrator. One does not respond, in other words, to physical punishment or its implied threat in the form of an inanimate object in the same way that one responds to the expectations of other individuals toward oneself. This is so because we live, work, and play largely with a view toward others' acknowledgment and acceptance of our activities. In the process, we depend upon them for an important part of the definition of our existence, just as, in turn, other individuals and groups live for and depend upon us for acknowledgment and attendant definition of their existence. The attachments stemming from these dependencies thus have their basis in the essence of the human condition; it is through their exercise and function that we attain our "humanness." What it means in part to be a human being is to be morally obligated to one's fellows—hence, the potential force of the concept of human responsibility, and the reasons why responsiveness to inanimate objects differs so fundamentally from responsiveness to the expectations of others. Indeed, because the response to a physical object such as a cane is so decidedly one way, it cannot even be said to be a responsiveness in the sense of moral obligation. One is not obligated to a physical instrument in the way one is obligated to one's fellows. For moral responsibility implies, by definition, a response in return. And it does not make sense to speak of one's being either responsive or responsible to a cane in the sense that one is to one's fellows. Hence—the cane's potential for bonding boy to master possibly seen as a special case—there is no responsiveness toward a cane in any moral sense; there is only a reaction to its implied threat,

150

or to some master at the moment of its administration. But let the master without whom the cane cannot act leave the room and what happens? Either the defenseless, inanimate cane is stolen, or better yet "mangled" or bent at right angles, or the boys—lacking self-discipline—make noise, waste time, or simply "raise hell."

The policy and practice of corporal punishment at Boys' High thus is incompatible with the professed aim of instilling in boys a sense of self-discipline and responsibility. Rather, the most that can be said of the cane is that it is convenient; it serves to relieve boys' and masters' frustrations; it can effect a bond between boys and masters and, in a different sense, the school; it is a sign of status to some, a signification of failure to others; it is all these and more. But it is not, in the final analysis, an effective instrument of self-discipline. On that score, its use in the school as an instrument of "discipline" must be questioned.

"Boys' Best Interests"

While neither masters nor parents can be accused of wilful insincerity of purpose toward the young, nor of having anything at heart but "boys' best interests," it may be that they are guilty of a kind of short-sightedness. Parents, and to no less an extent masters, seem to think that like "that old-time religion," you just can't get enough of that good old-fashioned discipline. Discipline appears to be almost everyone's answer to most problems of youthful unrest and protest. The seeming aim of elders' insistence on the need for ever-increasing doses of discipline—coupled with a fairly characteristic attitude that young people don't know enough yet to decide things for themselves—is to force boys to the point where, as the Headmaster once put it, "They don't even think about doing something silly." Rather, they are meant just to respond, in almost conditioned fashioned where certain matters are concerned.

Obviously there is a kind of value indoctrination going on here. The extent to which such indoctrination is desirable is debatable, of course, as is the extent to which it can be expected to work in these changing times. But as for the elders themselves, this much surely can be said. They talk a good game, perhaps even unknowingly. They speak as if genuinely desirous—as they doubtless are—that the youth conduct itself in a responsible, self-disciplined manner; yet they advocate policies and practices that appear to deny youth this very opportunity. They say to the young, on the one hand, "Grow up." Then, on the other hand, they speak and behave as though they are reluctant to see them do so. They call for increased communication, but are quick to blame the lack of it on television, or they deplore the "friendliness" of the few masters who try to enhance the flow of communication toward the boys in an effort to come to know them better. There is precious little recognition that genuine communication implies the capacity to listen. They talk of the need for discipline so as to "make" the youth behave themselves, but draw little or no distinction between externally imposed discipline and self-discipline. If and when they do note a difference, the presumption is that more of the former insures more and better of the latter. And yet in all of this, elders see themselves as having only boys' best interests at heart. That is why they cannot be accused of wilful insincerity of purpose; they can only be charged, perhaps, with myopia. The end effect of their nearsightedness, of course, can be the same in either case.

The boys, understandably, are as oblivious to inconsistencies of this sort as their elders. They, too, sense little contradiction in their approval of so potential a suppressant of self-discipline as the cane and their repeated cries for increased opportunities to engage in self-responsible practices:

> "This school doesn't exist for the boys in it," he noted acidly. "The boys don't matter." "That's right," piped in still another. "This school is like a little computer. This school doesn't let you develop your own thought processes. You don't get any opportunities to practice responsibility." Capping this outburst of dissatisfaction, one boy added somewhat more thoughtfully than the others, "From Fifth Form on we're supposed to be getting ready to take jobs and be adults. But we don't get the chance to think and act for ourselves—not even in Sixth Form."
> I must note at this stage how consistently, of late, I have been impressed by Fifth and especially Sixth Form boys' complaints about the inopportunity to practice self-responsibility. It is a frequent criticism, coming even as it did today from a group of boys at the lower end of the academic spectrum—athletes in the main, and second-time-around UE boys—lads from whom one would expect to hear, last of all, a concern with the lack of opportunity to practice some form of self-responsibility. But while they cry on the one hand for opportunities of this kind, they decry on the other any suggestion that corporal punishment be abolished —blind to any connection between the cane as a suppressant of self-discipline and their alleged desire to engage in self-responsible practices —blind to the incompatibility, if not contradiction in terms, of an authoritarian model of education and their expressed wish to engage in self-responsible practices.
>
> SIXTH FORM BOYS, SEPTEMBER 1969

Of the many boys I encountered, only one even vaguely sensed the conflict in boys' acceptance of the cane as measured against their complaints that "this school doesn't let you develop your own thought processes." And that boy, interestingly enough, was the one American attending the school:

152

From the general tone of his remarks, it was plain that Doug harbored no ill feelings about the cane, even though he spoke as one who—unlike his peers—had not grown up with corporal punishment in the schools. He gave every appearance of having "adjusted." Yet, unlike his classmates, he had at least seen beyond these walls and was thus in a position to conceive of alternatives. Consequently, he made a criticism which I had not once heard from the Kiwi lad: "I don't mind the cane. I've grown accustomed to it. I even think that in some ways it's good. It's quick." Pausing a moment, he added by way of afterthought, "But it doesn't leave a lasting impression on your mind—not like a verbal talking-to, which makes you think about what you've done."

FIFTH FORM BOY, AUGUST 1969

If there is reason to suspect the cane's utility as an instrument of self-discipline, there is less doubt concerning its capacity for instilling attitudes of unquestioning submissiveness and unreflecting obedience to authority. From all appearances, the cane is intended to instill in boys in totally unreflective fashion the so-called "true values" in life. That it *does* instill values of one kind or another—at least for a time—is not unlikely; that it provides boys with an appreciation of these values in any lasting sense is less likely; that the values instilled are, indeed, "true" values is another question still; but it is a question which boys are seldom permitted to entertain. The aim is not so much to have them reflect upon these values, but rather to insure that they "get" them. For on the view of most elders, boys this age really are not in a position to reflect on these things even if they had the desire.

Ultimately, perhaps, the decision whether or not to employ the cane hinges on one's answer to the questions: At just what age, or at what stage in their young lives are boys in a position to begin to reflect on such matters as the true values in life, to learn them in a fashion that bespeaks genuine meaning rather than to have them "whacked" into them? Can, in fact, such personal attributes as honesty, courage, and integrity be pounded into a boy? Or does one attain these attributes in other ways? And if the cane is not instilling in boys these things because it is inherently incapable of doing so, what then is it doing? Can a responsible parent or master insist on certain forms of conduct for the young whether the young can appreciate it or not? When are these same elders irresponsible for insuring too much in the young's so-called "best interests?" Is a secondary school like Boys' High in the business of instilling in boys "true values," whatever the price and whatever the method? Or is it involved with helping boys begin to learn how to reflect upon and decide things for themselves? Or is it in the business of doing both or neither of these things? These are the kinds of questions on which the issue of corporal punishment at Boys' High may well hang.

153

Let the further question be raised: Are these questions—or any like them—even being discussed at Boys' High? One has to conclude they are not. Too concerned with belting the starch out of the more spirited boys in their own best interests, often too busy wtih the strict maintenance of order, too overburdened, possibly, with extra-curricular duties and irrepressible lads, too pressured on all sides, perhaps, by the overwhelming constraints of the system itself, basically content to accept rather than question that system, most masters—and for other reasons, most parents—supposing they had the inclination, have neither the time, the needed effort, nor the purpose of will to pursue the answers to such questions in more than passing fashion. Such, perhaps, is the lot of the teacher. Who has time, after all, to be bothered with academic questions thrown out from some distant ivory tower when there is so much practical work to be done?

Of all the masters I encountered, only one volunteered a suspicion that caning might hinder the development of self-discipline and initiative of thought:

> "Corporal punishment," he stated thoughtfully. "That's a dicey one. I don't like it, though I use it myself sometimes. It worries me . . . more as I get older . . . mostly for this mental attitude it instills in boys . . . the boys expect it . . . they just take it as a natural part of things. If they do something wrong, they expect to get walloped. I use it sometimes in sheer desperation. The place just calls out for it . . . it's so strong here . . . I think a good blow-off at them is more effective, but sometimes after a boy has done something wrong, and he knows I'm angry, he'll say to me, 'Why don't you belt me?' as though this makes everything right again. He thinks it absolves him of blame, takes the blame off him, whereas it only leaves things unresolved. He's got to feel the blame . . . caning is just an external form of discipline. I don't think it teaches self-discipline . . . but mostly it is this military mentality that it implies—this obedience to orders without any question."
>
> JUNE 1969

The Boys: A Final Note

One of the redeeming features of the system (or its potential ruin) may well be the boys themselves. Blind though they may be to certain inconsistencies in their own thinking, they are not altogether mindless of the school's shortcomings. Indeed, when they *are* given opportunities to express their opinions, they usually have lots to say. Moreover, their criticisms, however imperfect, are an indication of insight and maturity. Nothing better illustrates this than one Sixth Form boy's essay, "Reasons

Why I Am at This School." While the exercise was assigned by the First Assistant as penalty for some indiscretion, in fairness to the administration it should be recognized that these essays provide the older, more mature boys opportunities, however limited, to "have at" the system. By the same token, they are a convenient, institutionalized channel of socially sanctioned defiance, one of the system's several "safety valves." One hopes that just as boys are capable of recognizing in some masters that "he cared enough to give me a hiding," masters in turn will recognize in essays such as this, and "Courtesy," that the boys, after all, are mature enough and care enough about Boys' High to give the system an occasional "hiding" of its own:

Reasons Why I Am at This School

The reason I am at this school is not to be educated, nor to gain moral standards, but merely to gain sufficient academic qualifications to enable me to be educated at university, and in the process pick up the basic knowledge required for it.

The reason I chose this school was not for its good name, nor its long tradition (for these I would have gone to another school), but for its good pass rates in the national exams (S.C., U.E., Bursary, and Scholarship).

Since I wish to obtain certain qualifications, I am obliged to obey the school rules, under threat of expulsion. I am quite ready to obey the school rules—if I only knew where I could obtain a copy. There seems to be a great lack of any form of written rules dealing with domestic matters and one would wonder if there are any. If there are some then I would like to know on whose standards and values these rules are based. Surely a poll on the general public's opinion of school dress and discipline would be more "democratic" than a mandatory ruling by the school board.

Under the present education system, state schools are here merely to educate people, not to teach them standards of behavior and moral values. A state school can not hope to impress ideals upon young men attending the establishments due to the innate impersonality of the system. High school sees the change of boys to men and hopes to broaden their outlook as they mature. In doing so these young men realize the fallibilities of the system by which they are being taught. It is a vicious circle—like the dog biting the hand that feeds it—because the hand is also trying to slip a collar on the dog as it feeds it.

Of course, there are the beautiful ideas of—you can't take all the time, you must give—and—while you are here you will do as we tell you and if you don't like it you can leave. These appear ostensibly to be justifiable, taken as they appear, but when one applies them to the present social beliefs one can see the fallacies in the argument. In the first it is just like business; unless you have a lot of capital you cannot start, and the loans can be payed back when you have gained enough money; in this case you must take before you can give and this is what my generation is doing, whereas your generation is giving back what it took when it was young. In the second case it is like the man holding the bone in one hand and the big stick in the other while the starving dog cringes before. The school has what we want and while we are begging and scraping to get these, the school can deal a few blows and poke us a bit. Why? The reason is as incomprehensible as why the big man must beat the dog.

Unfortunately although I don't like the school system, being so impersonal and condescending, I do like what we are taught and generally respect the people who teach me. Although some of my reasons for attending this school are not entirely selfless they are nonetheless true. Basically I feel the school has something to offer, but I do not feel it is a gift but a right.

UPPER SIXTH FORM BOY, JULY 1969

Which Kind of Society? What Kind of Product?

Just as one has to look at some of the things going on *beyond* the school in order to better understand some of the things going on *inside* it, the question of the cane's employment ultimately has to be considered in terms of the interests and objectives of the larger community. That is to say, the question "To cane, or not to cane?" cannot be adequately dealt with prior to a consideration of the *kind of society*—and the role of the individual in that society—that one has in mind.

Does one, for example, want as a product of the educational system individuals who are inclined to conform passively to the system, to accept its authority without much question in the interests of maintaining order, stability, and the status quo? Or does one want citizens who tend to raise serious, hopefully responsible, but just as likely, troublesome, if not altogether subversive questions about the system's functions and objectives? The choice is not an easy one, any more than it is the only one. Neither situation, in its extreme form, is especially attractive—the one hinting of social stagnation and dullness, the other of social chaos. But for that reason alone, it is worth considering the point along the continuum where one's society ought to be situated given the social, economic, and political requirements of the times.

As but one aspect of that consideration, it is suggested that a system of corporal punishment, in association with an authoritarian model of education, engenders in pupils neither self-discipline nor a particularly responsible attitude toward one's societal obligations generally. Rather, it appears to have an opposite effect—namely, the creation of attitudes of overdependency and unquestioning submission to one's superiors in the latter's presence, as against defiance and disrespect for authority in their absence. Ausubel notes:

156

The survival of a self-perpetuating (authoritarian) training system that was incongruous with the general tenor of interpersonal relationships and behavioural standards in the culture at large created many serious problems, chief among which was the development of an adult personality with an immature, resentful and overconforming attitude toward authority. . . . Overtraining in overt but resentful deference to an outmoded authoritarian discipline that he cannot fully internalize thus sets the pattern of the New Zealand adolescent's response to authority which he carries with him into adult life. When confronted face-to-face with the arbitrary pronouncements of officialdom, instead of questioning their wisdom and challenging them publicly, the adult New Zealander tends to comply with little or no open show of protest. . . . he seems to be genuinely overimpressed with the omniscience of authority figures, and to believe that they are really wiser than he. Intellectually, of course, he may think that they are all wrong, but emotionally he stands in awe—as a child—of their right to make unchallengeable decisions, and cannot bring himself to demur in their presence. This attitude is undoubtedly the upshot of years of conditioning to an arbitrary, overbearing and heavy-handed authority at home and in school that brooks no opposition and demands unquestioning compliance . . . But when he does not have to deal directly with authority, he may either evade it surreptitiously, challenge it symbolically, or make use of institutionalized channels of socially sanctioned defiance.[6]

Harold Bourne carries the case a step further:

In his dealings with authority, I would say, the New Zealander knows only two maneuvers—flat disregard when unseen, and passive compliance otherwise. Typically he seldom questions authority, and he never opposes it head on, but if its back be turned, he follows his own inclinations. His passivity can readily be demonstrated—just suggest challenging a decision from Wellington! The dictates of officialdom which, in England, would be met by a furious letter to one's M.P. and a phone call to a newspaper don't even arouse indignation here. The innocent objector is told, "Oh! But that comes from Wellington," and ultimately he gathers that "Wellington" is no more to be shifted than the sun. As for evading authority when concealed, this is done as a simple matter of course. There is a 50 miles per hour speed limit, but the country roads can't be closely patrolled so many ignore it; after-hours trading is illegal, but inspectors can't be everywhere, so the grocer will oblige; it is an offense to feed dogs raw offal, but no one can ever be caught, and so hydatid disease is as prevalent as before the regulation. In short, the New Zealander is both a tame conformist and an habitual law-breaker, but the third course, changing the decree, seldom occurs to him—he is not a reformer and he is not a radical.[7]

In other words, an authoritarian model of education—a system of corporal punishment only its most visible mode of enforcement—

[6] *The Fern and the Tiki*, pp. 85, 111.
[7] From a talk entitled, "The Family," given by Harold Bourne, Lecturer in Psychiatry at the University of Otago Medical School, 1958.

ironically gives every indication of having an exactly opposite effect than that intended. Rather than inculcating qualities of self-discipline, critical judgment, and initiative of thought, it appears to create attitudes of over-dependency, hostility, aggressiveness, and unquestioning, unreflective submissiveness. In further support of this claim, one notes an interesting experiment on the effects of authoritarianism as described by Stone and Church. In this experiment,

> . . . adult leaders worked with three groups of ten-year old boys formed into clubs to carry on such activities as theatrical mask-making. To eliminate the effects of personality differences among the leaders, each adult assumed in rotation autocratic, democratic, and "laissez-faire" roles carefully worked out in advance. Each group of boys was exposed to all three types of leadership, but no group ever had the same leader playing different roles. . . . The experiment yielded a wealth of findings; here we shall be concerned only with those having a bearing on education. Quantitatively, both the autocratic and democratic groups were equally productive, while output in the "laissez-faire" group was low. Qualitatively, however, the work of the democratic group was superior to that of the "laissez-faire" or the autocratic group. In the course of the project, the "laissez-faire" group lost interest, and its activities became desultory, with considerable horseplay. The presence or absence of the leader made little difference. In the authoritarian group, the maintenance of production apparently depended on pressure from the adult leader, for, when he left, work tended to cease. In the democratic group, interest and motivation remained high, and even when the leader was absent, work went on in the established pattern. Even more significantly, members of the authoritarian group either became indifferent and apathetic or developed rather intense aggressiveness. . . . Besides the work stoppages that occurred every time the autocratic leader left the scene, there was a cork-out-of-the-bottle effect: all sorts of feelings, largely hostile, exploded. This behavior may be evidence of the strain generated in children by rigid external controls of this kind, and may be compared to the way children explode out the doors at three o'clock from schools where they are similarly held in check. Significantly, a similar explosion took place when groups changed from authoritarian to democratic leadership. A comparable phenomenon is likely to appear when schools make the change from authoritarian to democratic organization, often leading to the belief that the rigid controls of the old regime were really necessary to maintain discipline.[8]

Anderson suggests:

> Rigorous discipline, with close controls, tends to make an adult who is a good "obeyer" because it decreases spontaneity, initiative, and per-

[8] L. Joseph Stone and Joseph Church, *Childhood and Adolescence* (New York: Random House, 1957), pp. 260–62.

sistence. By giving a child opportunities for initiative, spontaneous action, and choice, the possibility increases that he will show the qualities making for effective leadership.[9]

And finally, in a previously cited article entitled, "Research Facts About Corporal Punishment Which Many Ignore," Michael Sequin concludes:

> . . . research involving children has shown not that punishment, corporal or otherwise, is a sensible, harmless and effective method of behavior control, but rather that punishment creates anxiety which decreases school achievement, has no "example setting" power, and produces children who are aggressive, narrow-minded, uncreative, over-dependent and irrational.[10]

Research thus suggests that a system of corporal punishment, in conjunction with an authoritarian model of education, infringes on the individual pupil's potential for self-disciplined, self-responsible conduct by conditioning him to expect not only to be hold *what* to do, but *how* to do it. If, in the end, pupils are better, or at least none the worse for their experiences under such a system, one suspects this is in spite of, rather than because of the institution of corporal punishment and the authoritarian atmosphere of the school overall. And even then, one wonders what might have been the effect on these same students under the guidance of a democratic rather than an autocratic system.

It is worth noting, in this regard, the observations of a former master of Boys' High School, the same individual who on page 82 said of corporal punishment, "Oh, I'm not all that against it—it didn't leave any permanent scars on me." Reminded of his earlier remarks upon reading the manuscript of this study, he wrote to me in January 1972:

> I am embarrassed now that I should have said so glibly, when you first talked to me, that I didn't think being caned had done me any permanent psychological harm. I guess I still don't think of it as having done me quite "harm." I mean simply that I don't think I'm pathologically anything because of being caned. But I am forced to admit that it did influence the formation of my present character or personality in ways that I had not recognized until I had read your study, and in ways I am increasingly thinking were not beneficial.

The inhibiting potential of a system of corporal punishment may be but the most obvious indication of a fundamental weakness of any school with an examination-oriented syllabus and an inordinate emphasis on

---

[9] John E. Anderson, *The Psychology of Development and Personal Adjustment* (New York: Henry Holt, 1949), p. 355.

[10] *Op. cit.*, p. 229.

academic achievement, and where an authoritarian model of education seeks absolute adherence to its standards while simultaneously professing as one of its objectives the instillation of self-discipline. One of the dangers in this, it would seem, is that out of reluctance to risk the slightest deviation from the norm, one runs the greater risk of the submissive, conforming, self-centered pupil who, anxious not to "rock the boat" in the interests of proper certification, is a perfectly tractable, docile, law-abiding citizen, but at the same time uninterested in anything except his own affairs. He may well be the real drag on the system, perhaps not so much at school—where certification via examination is of prime concern to all—but later as an adult member of the community. He may then come to be regarded—as Pericles suggested 2,400 years ago—not so much "quiet" as "useless."

There is no denying that we all have to learn to submit to some form of authority sooner or later; thus one may take the position that it *is* desirable in the preparation of the young for participation in adult society that they *are* inculcated with a strong respect for authority, even if to make the point stick early in the game, such respect takes the form of unquestioning subservience to one's "masters." But if this statement is true, it must be viewed with misgivings. For, as one New Zealand schoolteacher put it:

> . . . if we aspire to a democratic social order, we must aim at developing within each individual the capacity for self-regulation and self-direction of his conduct. Discipline, then, becomes not a matter of submissive obedience to authority—the passive good conduct which continual threats and dire punishment compel—but rather the voluntary or self-discipline which guides the individual and directs his conduct without their aid. Furthermore, if so much emphasis is placed on submissive obedience, it shows a disastrous lack of interest in the needs of our young, for it is much easier for the parents and teachers to give commands than it is to use the ingenuity required for intelligent control.[11]

Nor is the matter as uncomplicated as the preceding passage suggests. There is a great deal of appeal in Murdoch's assessment as well:

> The high school community is an abnormal society, in that it comprises a few adults and a large number of adolescents; that to the former belongs ultimate authority and responsibility, however this may be disguised; that it lacks the economic complications of the outer world; that its central purpose is clearly known and expressed, and involves the disciplining and training of the young; that it is a part-time institu-

[11] Richard Goldsmith, "More Thoughts on Discipline," *New Zealand Post-Primary Teacher's Association Journal*, XIV (July 1967), p. 15.

tion only, a temporary grouping for a specific purpose; and so on. . . . The adolescent, because he is an adolescent—that is, in the stage of becoming an adult—needs, and looks for, a measure of direction and firm and stable control. It is possible to be premature in the granting of authority or freedom. The best preparation for a normal manhood is, after all, a normal childhood and adolescence; and the nature and amount of freedom to be granted must be relative to the situation, and to the powers of the people concerned.[12]

To accept Murdoch's claims is not at the same time to excuse the authoritarian tone of Boys' High. Rather it is to suggest, as does Murdoch, that schools are peculiar institutions; that they are not necessarily replicas in miniature of the larger community even as they adjustively respond to the demands and expectations of that community; that they need not, therefore, always conduct themselves in ways that would appear to duplicate the practices of the larger community as though this implied preparation for participation in the world of adulthood. Each school must adjust to its particular circumstances in its own way, given the combined needs of the school and its community.

It is a condition of proper adjustment between school and community, however, that its basis be subject to occasional scrutiny. For its part, Boys' High School does not think to question seriously the basis of its relationship to the larger community, or whether the school itself is sufficiently in touch with the times. Nor does it indicate much willingness to readjust merely because—as Bob Dylan tells us in song— "The times they are a'changing." Rather, like Mitchell's "unthinking, untroubled man," Boys' High goes on doing mostly what it always has done for the simple, but appealing reasons that (1) "it works," [13] and (2) its conduct is consistent with the kind of attitudes toward it of the larger community which imply a preference for the unimaginative, the safe, the traditional. [14]

On the other hand, the failure of the school seriously to question itself probably has been—at least until now—one of its strengths. Boys' High obviously has shown itself to be efficient. Moreover, it has achieved

[12] J. H. Murdock, *The High Schools of New Zealand, A Critical Survey* (Christchurch, New Zealand: Whitcombe and Tombs Ltd., New Zealand Council for Educational Research, Series No. 19, 1943), p. 450.

[13] ". . . as long as things appear to be working satisfactorily the New Zealander seems to be completely satisfied to let them be, 'to let sleeping dogs lie.'" David Ausubel, *The Fern and the Tiki*, p. 35.

[14] "We are a conventional people, and distrust originality—especially in our preachers and teachers. So our education remains largely schooling, and touches little on actual life, and our schools are predominantly State schools, centrally controlled and supervised. We praise, but distrust youth; and our important positions are held by the old, the tried, the safe. We still prefer the instruction of youth to its encouragement in creative endeavor." J. H. Murdoch, *op. cit.*, p. 436.

the kind of results which everyone expects of it. No wonder its policy has been to turn out boys much in the image of their predecessors year after year. As with the enormously popular Volkswagen, the success of the school doubtless is due in part to its reluctance to alter the basic shape of its product.

But schools are not exactly like Volkswagen factories. Frequently conditions of a social and economic nature force changes upon them irrespective of their own desires, requiring them to re-tool and even to modify their product's basic shape. Mitchell puts forth the argument that indeed, the times are changing; that the path to New Zealand's future will be increasingly winding and complex, creating increased needs for persons with the capacity for independence of thought, critical judgment, and imaginative, forward-looking leadership:

> . . . the traditional pattern of our democracy has led to a deadlocked situation. Parties provide little dynamic, politicians accustomed to responding to popular demands have no clear goals, and the public provides no guidelines. The system can change and adjust to new circumstances, but it needs leadership, expert skills and a public awareness rather than the quick grasp of the practical which has characterized the past.
> New Zealand democracy has fought a long rearguard action against the emergence of an elite, which has been associated with privilege. It has insisted on politicians who do not stand out from ordinary mortals. It has looked to the man of general knowledge and skill at improvisation rather than to the specialist. The nation's destiny has been to export first-class brains and would-be specialists and import second-class ones and tradesmen: brains for brawn is the barter. Yet today the increasing sophistication of the machine and the increasing difficulty and complexity of its problems create an expanding role for the expert and the specialist. This in turn leads to an emerging function for an elite, qualified by intellect and ability, to control them and lead public opinion.[15]

And Ausubel notes:

> The honeymoon of prosperously muddling through while recklessly violating every known principle of economics is over. The current business recession is not just a temporary setback brought on by overspending of foreign exchange and the fall in wool and dairy prices. In the immediate future these prices will probably improve; but over the long haul the economic crisis will progressively deepen until New Zealanders are finally willing to face up to the one inescapable reality of economic life, namely, that to stay in business one must be able to compete effectively in a competitive world market. This requires enterprise,

---

[15] Austin Mitchell, *Politics and People in New Zealand* (Christchurch, New Zealand: Whitcombe and Tombs Ltd., 1969), p. 316.

efficiency, high productivity of labour, a forward-looking approach, long-term planning, and willingness to come to grips with and adapt to ever-changing world conditions.[16]

Add to this the fact of Britain's pending entry into the European Common Market, accompanied by the likely loss of New Zealand's "special position," and Ausubel's forecast of economic crisis appears to have been not far off the mark.[17]

For 10 years New Zealand has lived with the fear that the basis of her prosperity could be wrecked if Britain entered the European Economic Community without special provision being made for New Zealand products.

This week Britain's negotiations to join the market made sudden progress on several major issues and concern was growing here that Britain might come to terms that would give New Zealand little real protection.

For 90 years in peace and war New Zealand has functioned essentially as a big meat, wool and dairy farm whose produce has won guaranteed access to the British market. When it became apparent during the sixties that Britain might join the Common Market, the prospect caused near panic here.

Before World War II, 84 per cent of all New Zealand exports went to Britain. The figure today is 36 per cent. But 90 per cent of the butter, 78 per cent of the cheese and 88 per cent of the lamb still go to Britain. All these exports would be seriously threatened if Britain entered the market without special terms for New Zealand.

Thus far the British Government has held out for terms acceptable to New Zealand. It wants existing quantities of dairy produce to be admitted for a five-year period with provision for subsequent review. But the Common Market, and especially France, has declined to consider anything like such liberal terms.

Assurances given by the British Government to New Zealand have been such that a complete rebuff to New Zealand could hardly be contemplated, especially as New Zealand's claims are viewed sympathetically in Britain. But with most of the key issues already settled, fears are growing here that Britain might salve her conscience with face-saving measures.

The Prime Minister, Sir Keith Holyoake, and the leader of the Opposition, Norman E. Kirk, have spent the last month campaigning in Britain and Europe. When Mr. Holyoake returned here this week, Mr. Marshall made a hurried departure for Europe. It is widely believed here that the crucial stage is now at hand and the greatest test of New Zealand's persuasive powers is about to begin.[18]

[16] David Ausubel, *op. cit.,* p. 228.

[17] It is true that Britain's application to join the European Common Market was amicably received in 1971. But actual membership on a working basis probably is several years' away. In the meantime, British entry must still be regarded as pending.

[18] "Trade Issue Stirs New Zealanders," *New York Times,* May 16, 1971, p. 9 (Special to the New York Times from Auckland, New Zealand, May 15).

Caning is a ritual—one which goes on and on and on. The faces change, but the roles remain. Like most rituals, it serves as a thermostat. It tries to keep the system in balance, to maintain the old working-class values of discipline, manliness, and egalitarianism. The interesting consideration, however, is not so much the functioning of the ritual, or even its interpersonal or symbolic meaning to the participants, but rather the attempt to force upon ritual more than it can bear, the persistence of the ritual in the threat of change, and its acceleration of need before its ultimate demise. For caning will die. And it will die not because of will, but because of dramatic changes in the social order, changes desired by those same solid, middle-aged, middle-class types interviewed in Chapter 8 wanting more in the way of a material life. And "more" comes from machines and technologists and immigrants and "Yankee" and Japanese capital and technicians, and initiative and know-how, and the realization, as Ausubel has stated, "that to stay in business one must be able to compete effectively in a competitive world market." The ritual is subject to so much positive and negative feedback under these circumstances that it finally expires, it becomes dysfunctional, and new rituals take its place in the stream of time. The really important point of this study, therefore, is not that of boy, master, parent, and milieu as an interaction system around caning. The crucial problem is that of an elite school (by definition reactionary—it has more to lose) in a pastoral democracy "hell-bent" toward urban-industrial civilization. The real issue is social change and social ritual within a context of change, and how schools like Boys' High will adapt (or fail to adapt) to new circumstances.

The average New Zealander—pragmatic, but conservative—would not think to question seriously the basis of his system so long as it worked. Nor would the average boy, master, or parent of Boys' High think to question the purposes and function of the school—so long as everything worked. Rather, altered social, economic, and political conditions have begun to force these questions on them. Mitchell and Ausubel both have implied that the present situation has created increased needs for individuals possessing the qualities of critical thought, independence of judgment, imaginative leadership and a willingness to come to grips with and adapt to ever-changing conditions. These are not the products one associates, *prima facie,* with an authoritarian system of education. Rather, as has been suggested, such a system gives every indication of discouraging these qualities.

Alas, all too often, the basic issue has been distorted into a war between "discipline" and "permissiveness." The real issue is between vitality and stupor; between the maximization of human potential within the constraints of each life stage and the stifling of this potential by a repressive educational system which insists, above all, on absolute conformity to its standards.

One has to conclude that Christchurch Boys' High School—and in all likelihood, other schools in New Zealand much like it—is engaged in a desperate struggle to preserve the past and stave off the present. Like any socially created institution, however, it is only as viable as the system which made it, only as good as the class it was intended to serve. And both have plainly undergone appreciable changes since the school's founding in 1881. All the talk of "true values" and of the need to instill in boys "the essence of this school," all that stoic discipline, the inordinate emphasis on manliness, egalitarianism, and uniformity of attitude and appearance, may have justified themselves in a day when masters could take for granted their positions of authority and control, when the disciplinary policies and practices of the school were more in line with the needs and realities of adult life, and when boys themselves were content merely to be seen but not heard. But all that has changed.

> In former days authoritarian training was undoubtedly more effective than it is today in instilling ambition and conscientious work habits into New Zealand youth. Stern necessity not only made hard work an almost universally practiced virtue, but also created a Spartan social environment in which the authoritarian traditions of the Victorian era were not too incongruous with the newly espoused egalitarianism. With the passing of the frontier and the emergence of the Welfare State, however, authoritarianism consistently lost ground in adult society; as life became easier and less demanding, people found authoritarian practices increasingly less tolerable and less compatible with the egalitarian ideal. . . . Only the authoritarian flavour of the training system remained relatively unchanged. . . . it became solidly entrenched and resistive to change in the training system, acquiring considerable sacred cow status. . . . But in view of the wider cultural changes, youth could no longer implicitly accept either the justice of the discipline or the importance of practicing virtues that their elders disregarded. They became habituated to striving and working hard under external pressure but failed to internalize these values. Thus, when they finally entered the adult vocational world and the customary authoritarian demands for conscientious effort were lifted, the tenuous structure of their disciplined work habits tended to collapse in the absence of genuinely internalized needs for vocational achievement.[19]

When a peoples' myths, however cherished, have outlived their usefulness—as is the case both within and beyond Boys' High—when the

[19] David Ausubel, op. cit., pp. 49, 84–85.

old assumptions no longer are valid, then all dependent practices begin to smell of the vulgar, the arbitrary, the repressive. In the interests of its own coming of age, Boys' High would do well to concern itself less with the school's image, or with making old boys of young boys, or with disciplining pupils most of whom by virtue of their native intelligence, their parents' station in life, or, "that old school tie," will find good jobs and assume positions of leadership and responsibility in any case, and concentrate instead on encouraging young men in the exercise of those qualities which changed conditions will increasingly require of them in the days ahead.

Methodological Appendix

I. *The Technique of Participant Observation*

To understand the perspectives used by individuals in handling problematic situations is to grasp the situational symbols used by them in constructing relevant courses of action. One way to achieve such an appreciation is to take part in the everyday situations in which such symbols have meaning. This is not to suggest that one assume the stance of "objective observer." On the contrary, to try to capture the meanings inherent in the interactional process by standing back in the interests of objectivity and refusing to assume others' roles is to risk the worst form of subjectivism. On this approach, one is likely to substitute his own interpretation rather than to capture the meanings of things as they occur within the participants' range of experience. If one effectively is to come to terms with the situational symbols used by people in dealing with their everyday problems, then he has to take some part in these activities. Just as the participants interact with one another, so must the individual studying participants' perspectives interact with them. Just as the participants assume one another's roles in the process of adjusting to each other's attitudes and expectations, so must the person who wishes to document and explain the perspectives of the participants assume their points of view. For in the process of interacting with and taking the role of the people he is studying, the participant-observer recreates in his own thinking the same ideas and feelings—hence the symbols—which are in the minds of the participants themselves. And by symbolically interpreting people's perspectives, he comes perhaps as close as humanly possible to capturing the meanings of their ideas and actions as they would occur in real life.

Therein, too, lies the connection between the study's problem and the methodological approach to its investigation. The methodology is an outgrowth of the same concept of symbolic interaction as lies at the theoretical heart of the study's problem. To come to grips with peoples' perspectives is to take some part in their activities. One participates—physically and symbolically—as one observes. Hence the name of the method—participant observation. The study's problem and the study's methodological approach are linked within the same symbolic interactionist framework.

Apart from familiarizing myself as thoroughly as possible with the literature on participant observation prior to the study's initiation, I received no training—practical or otherwise—in this methodology. That is to say, I learned the method of participant observation "on the job."

An Appropriate Role

The adaptation of an appropriate role is essential to effective participant observation. The success with which the participant-observer performs his task hinges on the compatibility of his social role with the cultural standards and expectations of the people he is studying. Raymond Gold has suggested four theoretically possible roles for sociologists conducting field-work. These range from the complete participant at the one extreme, to the complete observer at the other.[1] The role chosen as being most compatible with the overall requirements of this study lay between the two, coming closest to what Gold calls, "the observer-as-participant." Accordingly, one observes as he participates, the emphasis being more on observation than participation. The role carries with it numerous opportunities for natural social interaction, yet has the advantage of permitting the researcher to terminate his interactions with his informants at will without threatening the genuineness of his relations with any of them. This is possible because his personal involvement with his informants retains sufficient elements of the "outsider" to avoid too intimate an attachment to any one of them. The field worker and those whom he studies are aware that theirs is basically a research, not a peer relationship. The researcher is thereby free to inform his subjects of as little or as much about his reasons for being there as he feels is desirable under the circumstances. He is also free to observe formally, as in scheduled interview situations, or informally, when attending social gatherings, for example. The observer-as-participant enjoys comparative freedom of movement among all of the participants, a necessity in situations where the participants hold contrasting points of view. At the same time, he maintains a genuinely human relationship with them, one that is both honest and sincere.

II. *Getting to Know the Participants*

A. *The Masters:* On the morning of my first full day at the school I was accompanied by the Headmaster to the staff room. Here the school's

[1] Raymond Gold, "Roles in Sociological Field Observation," *Social Forces,* XXXVI (March 1958), pp. 217–23.

teachers gather daily for a few brief minutes prior to school assembly and the start of classes. I was introduced to the staff by the Headmaster as Mr. Joseph Mercurio, a Fulbright scholar from Syracuse University who was interested in learning what made a school like Boys' High "tick":

> "Mr. Mercurio will be with us for at least several months," he explained. "I would appreciate your being of every possible assistance to him during that time."

MARCH 1969

Asked if I wished to say a few words on my own behalf, I took the opportunity to explain that mine was a somewhat different approach—that I was interested in looking at the school's policies and practices from the standpoint of its participants. I told the staff I hoped to accomplish this by participating as closely as possible in their lives, and in the lives of the school generally, ". . . even if this means getting out there on that huge sporting field of yours and learning how to play Rugby." The latter comment ended the introduction on a light note and was greeted by a round of good-natured laughter, hefty applause, and shouts of "Hear, hear." "Assembly," came a shout from the staff room door. With that, black-gowned masters, a Headmaster, and one slightly bewildered-looking "Yank" marched off to "Morning Assembly," a military-like gathering of the entire school body. I was introduced to the students much as I had been presented to the staff. The Headmaster urged the boys to be as cooperative as possible in the interests of the success of my study. The introduction was greeted by a sturdy round of applause, the school's traditional form of welcome.

I made a point of learning the first name of every master at the school within the first week of my arrival, much to the astonishment of several of them. It was meant to be an honest and sincere expression of my interest in them as individuals, and laid the foundation for a congenial and informative relationship.

Throughout the study, I never failed to ask a master's permission to visit his class, though there came a point when this probably was no longer necessary. I always assured them that I was not there to evaluate the quality of their teaching performance, which I wasn't. Rather, as I explained to them, I wished to gain an understanding of the conditions under which life at the school went on.

I adopted a quiet, inoffensive, unassuming role from the start. My instincts told me this was a time for feeling things out. Bold initiatives could wait. The prize to be gained by this approach was the trust and cooperation of the staff and greater freedom of movement within the school. I was still very much an outsider those first weeks and I knew it.

I avoided the role of "educational theorist," as it was obvious that

169

masters looked upon such individuals with suspicion. My teaching experience at the secondary level had long since acquainted me with most of a schoolteacher's problems and concerns. I used this knowledge to move into the role of "researcher-colleague," with a definite emphasis on the latter half of the title. I came to be seen as having a reasonably appreciative view of the complexities of a school from the standpoint of a teacher.

By the end of the third week I sensed increased acceptance by the staff. But I still was not sure. I finally took one of the masters into my confidence, telling him that as an outsider I was naturally concerned with how well I had been accepted:

> "You want to know how you've been accepted here," he said quite earnestly. "I'll tell you how. You've been very well accepted. I think you've gone about it in the right way. I remember you coming to my class the first time—to observe my teaching. You didn't throw yourself around like some. You've been very quiet, very conservative. Now I don't think you'll have any problems with a single person on this staff. I've heard nothing derogatory about you since your arrival."
>
> April 1969

That same week, in response to my statement that I hoped I was not an imposition, the First Assistant assured me:

> Well, I don't think I'm letting any secrets out of the bag. But most of the staff think very well of you. You've found a good little niche here. We've had people come to look at us for a day or two, but you're the first to come and have a real look at what makes us tick.
>
> April 1969

The content and style of my encounters with the staff varied considerably. I marched in with them at morning assemblies, attended morning and afternoon tea breaks, and ate lunch with them when I wasn't spending the day with the boys. Sometimes I would simply take a seat in the staff room while school was in session and either keep my eyes and ears attuned to whatever might be going on, or engage in a friendly conversation with anyone interested. Friday afternoon was a time for drinking beer, telling stories, and carrying on "discussions"—all within the relaxed atmosphere of Nancy's Pub, a favorite after-school haunt of the staff. I might add that some of the most valuable of the study's insights were obtained within the friendly confines of Nancy's.

In addition to participating in the life of the staff in largely group situations, I held private interviews—or "natters" as they came to be called —lasting approximately one hour. Over the nine-month period I was at

170

the school, I had "natters" with all but one of the school's 45 masters,[3] the complete administrative and clerical staff, and the head custodian. The conferences were open-ended and unstructured. This technique allowed me considerable flexibility. I was able to follow promising leads and test working hypotheses in a way that would not have been possible with a rigid scenario. I usually led off the exchange with the question: "What are some of the things that make your job here enjoyable (and unenjoyable)?" As the topic of corporal punishment rose infrequently on its own, I injected it with the question: "One of the practices at Boys' High that interests me as an American is caning. Quite frankly, I've an open mind on the subject. I would be interested in hearing some of your views on this matter." The question was purposely open. Masters were thus encouraged to discuss caning in a "natural" manner. I took their comments to be a reasonably honest indication of their feelings. In the interests of facilitating the conversation, I did not take notes during the interview. These were recorded immediately thereafter.

Throughout—as I subsequently learned—no one suspected my specific interest in corporal punishment. There were times, however, when I was not so sure:

> It was a typical Friday afternoon at Nancy's Pub. Some of the staff were reminiscing over retired or departed masters. The conversation now centered on one in particular, an old music master nicknamed "Cookie," who reputedly spurred singing during the morning assemblies to heights since unmatched. "Cookie" was notorious not only for inspiring boys to sing, but for his canings. "You see, Joe," old Ian explained, "he was nearsighted. So whenever he caned a boy, the poor lad practically pulled his coat over his head—for self-protection—'cause you could never be sure which end old 'Cookie' was going to hit." The amusing anecdote had us all roaring with laughter, and was followed by one master's joking suggestion, "You really should have written your thesis on caning, Joe." "Yes," I halfheartedly retorted, "that's a great idea."
>
> EXCERPT FROM FIELD NOTES, MAY 1969

Background information on masters (See chapter 2) was obtained by use of the following questionnaire.

[3] The one master to shirk an interview would respond to my requests with: "If you want to talk to me, you'll have to come down to Nancy's Pub." So in one sense, I probably held more "interviews" with this one teacher than with any of the others.

STAFF QUESTIONNAIRE

Name:_____

These are some questions which, in the interests of time, I was unable to ask during our personal interview period. Because this information is essential to the completion of my study project, I would appreciate your cooperation in completing the questionnaire and mailing it to me in the attached stamped envelope by November 1. Naturally, all of the information will be kept confidential. Kindest thanks for your assistance.

Joe Mercurio

A. *Formal Education*
   1. *Secondary schooling*

Name of school	*Boys'/ Co-ed.*	*No. of years*	*Forms completed*
_____	_____	_____	_____
_____	_____	_____	_____
_____	_____	_____	_____

   2. *Training college/University*

Name of college/ university	*No. of years*	*Major subject area*	*Degree/ Cert.*	*Year obtain.*
_____	_____	_____	_____	_____
_____	_____	_____	_____	_____
_____	_____	_____	_____	_____

172

B. *Teaching Experience*

Name of school	*Boys'/ Co-ed.*	*No. of years*	*Major subjects taught*
_____	_____	_____	_____
_____	_____	_____	_____
_____	_____	_____	_____

C. *Boys' High*

1. Present position, i.e., Maths. teacher,
   1st Assistant, etc.   _____

2. In terms of subject matter, how many *different*
   classes have you to prepare for each week?   _____

3. On the average, how many actual working periods
   do you teach per week?   _____

4. How many free periods have you per week?   _____

5. List by subject, form and stream, and size of class,
   the subjects you teach.

Subject	*Form & Stream*	*No. in class*
_____	_____	_____
_____	_____	_____
_____	_____	_____
_____	_____	_____

6. List any extra duties, i.e., Department Head, Rugby coach,
   camera club, etc.

   _____

   _____

D. *Personal Information*
   1. Military Experience:

      a. War service: Yes_____   No_____
        Dates inclusive_____   Rank_____

      b. Present military affiliation_____

   2. Married: Yes_____ No_____

   3. No. of chidren: Total_____ Boys_____ Ages_____
                                     Girls_____ Ages_____

   4. Your age_____

   5. Your father's occupation(s)_____

   6. Apart from any military service, have you had any overseas travel?

      Yes_____   No_____

      If "Yes," describe briefly the place, nature and duration of your trip, i.e., holidays, work, study, etc.

B. *The Boys*: Getting to know the boys was not at all the harrowing experience I had imagined. Prior to meeting with them, of course, I had every reason to expect the worst. I had been told by more than one person upon my arrival in Christchurch that the typical New Zealand schoolboy was reserved and reticent—especially with strangers. The school's Headmaster advised me that pupil-teacher relationships in New Zealand stood in sharp contrast to the more casual, easy-going pupil-teacher relationships he had witnessed in American schools.[4] I thus came to feel that I would have to be at my best if I were to breach the boys' exterior defenses and gain their confidence and acceptance.

For the first three days at the school I was assigned to Roger Cameron, a History master. It was Roger's responsibility to acquaint me with Boys' High and to help me get settled in. I used my time with him to observe classes, to meet more of the staff, to ask questions of a general nature, and to gain some overall impressions of the school's operation.

By the fourth day, I expressed an interest in meeting some of the boys:

> "You want to have a 'natter' with them?" Roger asked. "What's a 'natter'?" I asked, dumbfounded. "Oh," he laughed, "it means having a talk—man-to-man." "Kind of like what we'd call a bull session," I suggested. "Something like that," he nodded.
>
> MARCH 1969

The following day Roger turned over to me his top Upper Sixth Form History class ($U6_1$). As neither of us could be sure of the openness of the boys' response in Roger's presence, it was decided to leave me with them on my own. The field notes catch something of that first encounter:

> I introduced myself as an American who was interested in taking a good look at what made a school like Boys' High "tick." But more than that, I explained, I hoped to gain an understanding of the school by looking at it partly through the eyes of the people who were a part of it. This meant that I would have to be concerned not merely with the viewpoint of the masters, but equally important, with the views of the boys. "You're a rather important part of this place," I told them. "Without you, there would be no Boys' High." I further explained that I was deeply interested in them, their thinking, and their problems. They appeared to accept this as an honest expression of my intent. It struck them as novel to be given this kind of personal attention by an outsider. I let them know from the start that what went on between us was confidential. I then gave them an opportunity to ask me some questions about anything that came into their minds. They wondered if I found their uniforms strange. I answered, "Not really." "Why did you choose

---

[4] The Headmaster visited schools both in the United States and Europe in 1962 with the help of an educational traveling scholarship.

Boys' High for your study?" one wanted to know. "Because I thought it would be interesting to look at a boys' school. We haven't many single-sex schools in America," I explained. And when someone asked me if we had caning in America, I explained that we did in some schools, but that for the most part we did not, though we had "equally good substitutes." I then naively asked in return, "Is caning practiced here?" "Oh yes," Paul said, "you'll hear it in the halls. As Upper Sixth Formers we don't get it anymore, but its pretty common amongst Fourth and Fifth Formers."

Toward the end of our period-long discussion I told the boys that I would like to learn more about life at the school from their standpoint, and wondered if I could join them on their daily rounds. "Would this be O.K. with you?" I inquired expectatiously, knowing that a good deal of the project's success hinged on their answer. "Or would it seem strange to have me tagging along?" They looked at each other quizzically for what seemed to me like an eternity. Then Chris—self-nominated spokesman for the others—announced, "No. It wouldn't be too strange. Besides, it's the only way you'll get to know about us." I hoped at the time that I did not breathe too visible a sigh of relief.

MARCH 1969

For the next two days I accompanied the boys on their daily rounds, somewhat to the surprise of several masters. I attended classes with them, took breaks when they did, ate lunch in the relaxed, informal setting of the Drama Club Hut, and talked with them about whatever came up. It was an exciting time. It was an informative time. I was honestly surprised at how interested I could become in the boys and how seriously I began to take their problems and concerns:

These boys are just a bundle of feelings and impressions, some serious, some quite frivolous and amusing. They expressed a genuine interest in America, its schools, the violence, the size of the United States as compared with New Zealand. They spoke of Boys' High, of how archaic it was in some respects, of how great an influence was exerted on the school by a well-financed Old Boys' Association, and finally of how the Headmaster "must sign at least 7,000 documents a year." They spoke disappointedly about how lacking was New Zealand night life, and in particular about what a pity it was that the entire country "has no more than three bloody 'strip joints.' " They were intensely eager—like boys anywhere, I suppose—to tell an interested outsider about themselves, their exploits, their achievements. "Quite a contrast from the reserved, untalkative New Zealand schoolboy I had heard so much about," I tell myself.

EXCERPT FROM FIELD NOTES, MARCH 1969

I felt that I was off and running. I had gained the confidence of this group of boys and I anticipated no difficulties with any of the others.

My activities with U6$_1$ set the pattern for subsequent encounters with other boys. In all of this, the staff was wonderfully cooperative. I had only to ask a master if I could have a "natter" with his class in the interests of getting to know them better. I was never refused. I would then introduce myself to the class in much the way I had with $U6_1$. Sometimes the master would remain behind as an interested but non-participating bystander. Mostly (all but 5 out of a possible 23 such meetings) he left me alone with his class. For the first half of the period I let boys ask me anything they wished. This not only served to satisfy their curiosity about any number of things—me included—but also enabled me to establish an immediate working rapport with them. By the second half of the period they were enough at ease for me to ask them some questions of my own. "What are some of the things you like (and dislike) about this school?" I would inquire. The question was purposely general and open-ended, so as not to give anyone the feeling of being "pinned down." If the subject of corporal punishment arose of itself we discussed it. Usually it did. Otherwise, I did not push the exchange in that direction. Mostly, I let the conversation run as natural a course as possible. Interested as I was in the boys' perspectives on caning, I was equally concerned with their thinking generally. Their collected comments constituted in part their definition of the situation in relation to which corporal punishment obtained its meaning. Thus even those statements that did not bear directly on the subject of caning served an important purpose. Toward the end of the period I would express the desire to accompany five or six boys on their rounds. There was never a shortage of interested, enthusiastic volunteers. The word obviously had gotten out among the boys. I was "that interesting Yank bloke with the funny accent." I usually left it to the master to do the selecting.

I was best able to pursue the boys' perspectives on corporal punishment during the lunch hour. I seldom had to force the topic. The boys invariably raised an issue which invited discussion about the finer points of caning. Our meetings were open-ended and unstructured. I found this the most useful method of tracking down interesting leads and of obtaining the boys' views in as natural a manner as possible. The information gathered under these circumstances thus ranged over a wide area, but unfailingly was of relevance to the study's central problem.

The boys' occasional attempts to involve me in their criticisms either of masters or of some aspect of the school usually were met with the reply: "I'm sure you fellows will appreciate my reluctance to become too involved. Much as I am interested in your views, you must remember that as a guest of the school, I am not in a position to be actively critical." Not only did this satisfy them, but it made them realize that if I was unwilling to talk about the masters behind their backs, neither would I be talking to masters about boys behind theirs. This enforced their view of me as a trusted confidant.

I interviewed 23 out of a possible 37 classes in the above-described manner—meeting with boys an average of twice weekly. The project ranged over five months. There was no point in rushing. I purposely took time to reflect on my encounters and to entertain new, previously unconsidered hypotheses. Though it would have been possible to obtain 100 percent coverage of the classes, this did not appear to be necessary. The boys' views as expressed under these circumstances came to have a familiar ring. There was no reason to repeat the process endlessly. There were better ways to spend my time. I especially wanted to meet with parents, a project that would involve six to eight weeks of work.

Table 12 is a summary of my coverage of classes by form and stream. Only those classes marked by an asterisk were interviewed. In addition to class interviews, of course, I encountered boys regularly in a variety of other situations, mostly spontaneous, both in and out of school.

TABLE 12
Class Interviews by Form and Stream

Form	**Stream (descending order of ability)**								
Upper 6th	*1	2	*3	*4	*5	6			
Lower 6th	*1	2	*3	*4	5	*6	7	*8	9
5th	*A	*B	*N	J	*K	L	*M	*S	
4th	*A	B	*N	J	*K	L	*M		
3rd	*A1	A2	A3	*B1	*B2	*C1	C2		

* Indicates those classes interviewed by observer.

** Streams J, K, L, and M in the Fourth and Fifth Forms were not streamed academically.

C. *The Parents*: Parents were selected for interviewing as follows. The Headmaster chose from each of the five forms the names of six parents with whom he had had personal contact and who could therefore be relied on to have enough interest in the school to express views on it. The risk of bias in such cases appeared minimal.[5] Of these six from each form, I selected two at random (the first and fourth names on the list). Two more from each form were chosen by me again at

[5] Indeed, there was nothing in the course of the interviews that distinguished the parents suggested by the Headmaster from those chosen by me at random.

random from the boys' school attendance cards (the seventeenth and eighteenth names alphabetically from each of the five forms). The parents interviewed thus represented a reasonable cross section across all forms.

It should be mentioned that it would not have been possible to hold interviews with parents except for the cooperation and approval of the Headmaster. Quite aside from my own research interests, I went into parents' homes as an associate of the school. Or that, at least, was the way the Headmaster saw it. Had he thought that I would offend parents in any way with my questions, I would not have been granted permission to proceed with this portion of the study. A copy of the letter of introduction sent to parents under the signature of the Headmaster appears at the end of this section. It is an indication of the extent of the Headmaster's cooperation. Not one of the original twenty sets of parents contacted refused to grant me an interview. Most of them considered it an honor to be chosen from among so many parents. Others—mostly out of curiosity, as I subsequently discovered—merely wanted a chance to meet with "the Yank bloke at the school."

I met with parents in their homes, usually in the evening, at a time when both mother and father were available. The exchange normally lasted from one to two hours, depending on the degree of interest and enthusiasm shown. I employed the same open-ended, unstructured techniques used with boys and masters. I usually began the discussion with the question, "Perhaps you could tell me exactly why you chose to send your son to Boys' High rather than some other school?" From that point on the conversation was allowed to follow its own course. As often as not the subject of discipline arose of its own accord. The topic of corporal punishment, on the other hand, was not a contentious issue among parents, and thus arose considerably less frequently by itself. In these cases, I conveniently injected the topic into the conversation much as I had in my interviews with masters.

As I wanted to obtain as many complete statements from parents as possible, I took notes openly during the course of the interview. This did not appear to hinder anyone's response. Most parents regarded me as a "researcher" and seemed to expect me to record their comments from time to time. Asked, "Will it bother you if I jot down a comment or two as we talk?" one mother responded characteristically: "Not at all. How can you possibly remember all of this if you don't take notes!" As it was usually quite late in the evening by the end of the interview, I did not formally write up my observations until the following morning. The interviews ranged over a six-week period.

Dear Mr. and Mrs. _____:

This is to introduce Mr. J.A. Mercurio of Syracuse University, Syracuse, New York. Mr. Mercurio is in New Zealand under the auspices of the Fulbright Foundation, and for the past six months has been conducting an observational study of educational policies and practices at Boys' High School. Mr. Mercurio's study is part of a Ph.D. Thesis project in Education and has the sponsorship of the U.S. Educational Foundation in New Zealand as well as the approval of the Education Board and the University of Canterbury Education Department.

In the interests of expanding upon his understanding of educational policies and practices at Boys' High School I would like him to meet and speak with some of the parents of the boys in attendance—partly in an effort to see the School through parents' eyes. It would assist him greatly if you would grant him an opportunity to meet with you in your home during a time that is convenient. The discussion would be a short informal one (about 45 minutes) in which he would have a chance to talk with you on some of your views of Boys' High School.

He will be ringing you sometime soon to ask your permission to proceed with this plan.

Yours sincerely,

C.F.S. CALDWELL
Headmaster.

III. *Sample Items of Evidence For and Against the CIE/CIA Perspective*

A. *Positive Instances*
  1. *Masters*
When things get very out of control, it's the cane. Everyone knows it. It's as simple as that.

APRIL 1969

"How do you feel about the cane?" I asked. "I think it's uncivilzed," he replied. "I've only used it once this year." "Well," I asked, "you've been here three years now. How did you find it in your first year?" "Well, then I had to use it," he offered. "Even though you regard it as uncivilized?" I asked. "Yes," he stated. "Sometimes, especially when you're new, the boys can really get to you. When it reaches the point you take these problems home with you, when you find it begins to interfere with your private life, you say 'the hell with it.' It's the system here. That's what they use. That's what they expect. So, uncivilized or not, I use it."

APRIL 1969

When I first came here I didn't like caning. Now I take the view of the Head—you don't live by the cane; but you use it when you have to.

JUNE 1969

Jack McEntee walked up to Gerry Masters to announce that he'd just discovered some boys in the Baths Prefects Room, "tearing the place apart." Jack explained, "I took them all out and caned the whole bloody lot." Gerry expressed concern over the illicit use of the room and remarked: "We'll just have to make it a rule. Anyone caught in that room is caned." He then left to check the matter out personally.

MAY 1969

2. *Boys*

"You expect it. If I do something wrong, it's only fair that I get caned. . . . I think you respect the master more as a result." I asked them if they thought the boys generally bore any resentment toward it. One spokesman for the group said, "No. I don't think so . . . it should be kept. If it were abolished, some of us would run wild."

FIFTH FORM BOYS, JUNE 1969

I asked one boy if he regarded caning as humiliating. "Not really," he said. "Everyone takes their whacks. By the next day you forget it."

SIXTH FORM BOY, MARCH 1969

One of the lads in the group spoke up about an encounter with the cane two days earlier. I asked him what he had done. He told me: "Oh, I got caught kicking water at another boy. Mr. Morrison saw me from the upstairs window and came down and let me have it." "Did it do any good?" I asked. "Oh, yes," he stated earnestly. "I had it coming. I won't do it again."

THIRD FORM BOY, MAY 1969

"I don't like the way some masters cane first and ask questions later," he noted. "I mean they just see a pack of boys and come over and pick one out and cane him, and they may have the wrong one. I think they should talk first and try to find out who did the thing. Otherwise, it's not fair." "And if you *did* commit the offense," I said, "is it fair then?" "Oh, yes," he replied. "Then you should get caned."

FOURTH FORM BOY, MAY 1969

3. *Parents*

I'm all for it as long as a master does it. You know that if a master does it, he needs it. . . . I got it when I was a kid. It was alright . . . never did me any harm. If the offense is bad enough, I'm all for masters doing it.

FATHER, SEPTEMBER 1969

"How do you feel about caning at the school?" I inquired. "When it's controlled, certainly no problem at all . . . our boys have never complained." "Would you care to see it abolished?" I asked. "Never thought about it," he said. Asked under what circumstances he

181

would consider the cane an appropriate expedient, he said: "I'll tell you. Our boy was reported to the Headmaster for drinking on the train to Queenstown. Well he was caned. Mind you, he needed to be caned; first, to be reminded this wasn't the thing to do, second, it let the school down, third, it was not a thing to do in public, fourth, it was stupid, and finally, he deserved it."

FATHER, OCTOBER 1969

"I'm all for caning," Mrs. Johnson offered. "If they deserve to be caned they ought to be caned." Mr. Johnson added, "I think it's alright up to Fifth Form, but after that it's beneath their dignity." "What would be your reaction to those who favor the abolition of corporal punishment in the schools?" I asked. "I don't agree with that. I think they're in the minority," he stated.

NOVEMBER 1969

Caning certainly is a deterrent. . . . I'd prefer to see them go on caning. If a master thinks it's warranted, I'd trust the master's judgment.

FATHER, OCTOBER 1969

B. *Negative Instances*
   1. *Staff*
The cane? It doesn't work. I've thought a lot about this. . . . I remember what it was like when I was a boy in Scotland. There, it was the strap. It didn't do no good. I just did it again. . . . I've talked with these boys. They'd rather have a caning than a detention. Now what does that say for the cane?

JULY 1969

My job is to teach boys. And you aren't teaching them if you're caning them.

APRIL 1969

2. *Boys*
"Masters shouldn't cane boys," he said. I asked why. "If your parents don't beat you at home," he offered, "then masters shouldn't be allowed to cane you at school."

THIRD FORM BOY, MAY 1969

"It's a childish thing to do," he said. I told him, "Now you're speaking as a Sixth Former. How would you feel as a Third Former?" One boy replied, "Oh, Third Formers think the cane is a criminal offense," thereby suggesting how overawed Third Formers were with caning. "But by our age," he continued, "you feel there must be a more mature way of punishing—say, a detention or something." I said: "Well, you're Sixth Formers. You don't really have to worry about getting caned anymore, anyway." "That's not true," he shot back. "Mr. Connaly caned a couple of Sixth Formers yesterday who were only walking down the hall." Another piped in, "Some masters have got caning on the brain."

SIXTH FORM BOYS, JUNE 1969

3. *Parents*
On balance, it is a defeatist form of punishment. . . . in my four or five years of teaching, I don't recall once strapping a child. . . . it is the teacher who can't control a situation who has to use the strap or the cane. On balance, we'd say caning is a last resort, and an admission of failure to control by other means.

FATHER, SEPTEMBER 1969

I would say for most drastic things it should be retained. . . . it's a bit degrading both for a teacher and a child. In the latter years (of raising our child) I felt that if I belted a kid, it was most degrading. No, I don't think I really favor it at all. Something's lacking if a teacher has to cane.

MOTHER, NOVEMBER 1969

Bibliography

Documentary Sources:

Field Notes: March 1969–January 1970, 595 pages.
The Appearing Book, 1905–1955, 316 pages.
Caning Book for Masters, Vol. I, 1924–1963, 241 pages.
Caning Book for Masters, Vol. II, 1966 to present.
Christchurch Boys' High School Prospectus for 1969.
Christchurch Boys' High School, Headmaster's Report 1969.
School Rules.

Books:

Alpers, O. T. J. *Cheerful Yesterdays*. Christchurch, New Zealand: Whitcombe and Tombs, Ltd., 1930.

Anderson, John E. *The Psychology of Development and Personal Adjustment*. New York: H. Holt, 1949.

Ausubel, David. *The Fern and the Tiki: An American View of New Zealand National Character, Social Attitudes, and Race Relations*. New York: Holt, Rinehart and Winston, Inc., 1965.

Bandura, A., and R. H. Walters, *Adolescent Aggression*. New York: Ronald Press, 1959.

Barber, Bernard. *Social Stratification*. New York: Harcourt, Brace & Co. 1957.

Becker, Howard S. and Blanche Geer. "Participant Observation: The Analysis of Qualitative Field Data" in *Human Organizational Research,* edited by Richard Adams and Jack J. Preiss. Homewood, Illinois: Dorsey Press, 1960, pp. 267–289.

Becker, Howard, Blanche Geer and Everett C. Hughes. *Making the Grade: the Academic Side of College Life*. New York: John Wiley and Sons, Inc., 1968.

Becker, Howard S., Blanche Geer, Everett C. Hughes and Anselm L. Strauss. *Boys in White: Student Culture in Medical School*. Chicago: University of Chicago Press, 1961.

Bruyn, Severyn. *The Human Perspective in Sociology: the Methodology of Participant Observation*. Englewood Cliffs, New Jersey: Prentice Hall, 1966.

Cameron, William J. *New Zealand*. Englewood Cliffs, New Jersey: Prentice-Hall, 1965.

Cresswell, Douglas. *Eight Christchurch Schools*. Christchurch, New Zealand: The Pegasus Press, 1956.

Durkheim, Emile. *Moral Education,* edited by Everett Wilson. New York: The Free Press of Glencoe, 1961.

185

Geer, Blanche. "First Days in the Field" in *Sociologists at Work*. Philip E. Hammond, ed. New York: Basic Books, 1964, pp. 322–44.

Gilson, M. "Women in Employment" in *Social Process in New Zealand,* edited by John Forster. Auckland, New Zealand: Longman Paul Ltd., 1969, pp. 183–97. ·

Havighurst, Robert J. "A Comparison of New Zealand and American Children on Emotional Response and Moral Ideology," in *Studies of Children and Society in New Zealand*. Christchurch, New Zealand: Canterbury University College, Department of Education, 1954, Section VI.

————. "What Parents Expect of the Schools," in *Studies of Children and Society in New Zealand*. Christchurch, New Zealand: Canterbury University College, Department of Education, 1954, Section VII.

Hodgkinson, Harold. *Education, Interaction and Social Change*. Englewood Cliffs, New Jersey: Prentice-Hall, 1967.

James, Keith Franklin. *Corporal Punishment in the Public Schools*. Los Angeles: University of Southern California Education Monograph, Number 18, 1963.

Junker, Buford H. *Field Work*. Chicago: University of Chicago Press, 1960.

McGee, T. G. "The Social Ecology of New Zealand Cities," in *Social Process in New Zealand,* edited by John Forster. Auckland, New Zealand: Longman Paul Ltd., 1969, pp. 144–180.

Mann, Horace. *Lectures on Education*. Lecture 7, "On School Punishment," delivered in 1840, first published in 1845. Boston: Ide and Dutton, 1845.

Mead, George Herbert. *Mind, Self and Society,* edited by Charles W. Morris. Chicago: University of Chicago Press, 1934.

————. *The Philosophy of the Act,* edited by Charles W. Morris. Chicago: University of Chicago Press, 1938.

Mitchell, Alan. *84 Not Out*. London: Heunel Locke Ltd., in association with George G. Harrap & Co., Ltd., 1962.

Mitchell, Austin. *Politics and People in New Zealand*. Christchurch, New Zealand: Whitcombe and Tombs, Ltd., 1969.

Murdoch, J. H. *The High Schools of New Zealand, A Critical Survey*. Wellington, New Zealand: Whitcombe & Tombs Ltd., New Zealand Council for Educational Research, Series No. 19, 1943.

Oliver, W. N. *The Story of New Zealand*. London: Faber and Faber, 1960.

Roth, Herbert. *George Hogben, a Biography*. Wellington, New Zealand: New Zealand Council for Educational Research, Whitcombe and Tombs Ltd., 1952.

Sinclair, Keith. *A History of New Zealand*. London: Penguin Books, 1959.

Stone, L. Joseph and Joseph Church. *Childhood and Adolescence*. New York: Random House, 1957.

Vellekoop, Cora. "Social Strata in New Zealand," in *Social Process in New Zealand,* edited by John Forster. Auckland: Longman Paul, Ltd., 1969, pp. 233–71.

Whyte, William Foot. "Observational Field-Work Methods" in *Research*

Methods in the Social Sciences, edited by Marie Johoda, Morton Deutsch and Stuart W. Cook. New York: Dryden Press, 1951, pp. 393–514.

Journal and Magazine Articles:

Bevan-Brown, Charles Edmund. "Recollections by the Headmaster," *Boys' High School Magazine,* No. 30 (1904), 68–69.

Coolidge, F. "To Spank or Not to Spank," *California Teachers Association Journal,* 53 (October, 1957), 11–12.

Dolger, Laura and Janet Ginandes. "Children's Attitudes Toward Discipline as Related to Socio-Economic Status." *Journal of Experimental Education,* 15 (December 1946), 161–65.

Eckstein, M. A. "Ultimate Deterrents: Punishment and Control in English and American Schools." *Comparative Education Review,* 10 (October 1966), 433–41.

Eisenstadt, A. "Spare the Rod and Spoil/Save the Child?" *Grade Teacher,* 78 (February 1961), 11.

Esposito, Frank. "Spare the Rod?" *The Clearing House,* 34, No. 2 (October 1959), 95–6.

Fein, Leah Gold. "Evidence of a Curvilinear Relationship Between IPAT Anxiety and Achievement at Nursery School," *Journal of Clinical Psychology,* 19 (1963), 374–378.

Garber, Lee O. "When Is Corporal Punishment Lawful?" *Nation's Schools.* 65, No. 4 (April 1960), 100–106.

Gide, M. W. and T. A. Shellhammer, "Parents' Perceptions of School Discipline." *California Journal of Elementary Education,* 27 (August 1958), 28–36.

Gold, Raymond. "Roles in Sociological Field Observation," *Social Forces* 36 (March 1958), 217–23.

Goldsmith, Richard. "More Thoughts on Discipline," *New Zealand Post-Primary Teachers' Association Journal,* 14 (July 1967), 15–16.

Hogben, George. "In Memoriam: Notice to Thomas Miller," *Boys' High School Magazine,* No. 19 (Term 1, 1901), 7.

Kluckholn, Florence R. "The Participant Observer in Small Communities," *American Journal of Sociology,* 45 (November 1940), 331–43.

Kounin, J. S. and P. V. Gump. "Comparative Influence of Punitive and Non-Punitive Teachers Upon Children's Concepts of School Misconduct," *Journal of Educational Psychology,* 52 (February 1961), 44–9.

Lefkowitz, M., L. O. Walder and L. D. Eron. "Punishment, Identification, and Aggression," *Merrill-Palmer Quarterly,* Vol. 9, No. 3 (1963), 159–174.

Lewin, K., R. Lippet, and R. White. "Patterns of Aggressive Behavior in Experimentally Created 'Social Climates'," *Journal of Social Psychology,* 10 (1939), 271–99.

Mortimer, O. "Should the Teacher Use the Cane?" *Elementary English,* 39 (April 1962), 367–70.

"Most Superintendents Favor the Use of Corporal Punishment: Opinion Poll," *Nation's Schools,* 53 (July 1956), 57–8.

Mowrer, O. H. "A Stimulus-Response Analysis of Anxiety and Its Role as a Reinforcing Agent," *Psychological Review,* 46 (1939), 553–565.

Pavri, Dina M. Kumari. "Attitude of School Children Towards Punishment," *Educator,* 10 (1956), 233–40.

Purl, M. C. "Children's Perception of Adult Behavior," *California Journal of Elementary Education,* 28 (August 1958), 22–7.

Sequin, Michael. "Research Facts About Corporal Punishment Which Many Ignore," *National Education* (New Zealand), (June 3, 1969), 226–30.

"Swat Students Who Misbehave," School Administrators' Opinion Poll, *Nation's Schools,* 73 (February 1964), 58.

Symonds, Percival M. "What Education Has to Learn from Psychology," *Teachers' College Record,* 57 (April 1959), 449–62.

"Teacher Opinion on Pupil Behavior," *N. E. A. Research Bulletin,* 34, No. 2, (April 1956), 49–108.

Topp, R. F. "Teachers Should Not Spank School Children," *Educational Forum,* 24 (January 1960), 221–24.

Vidich, Arthur. "Participant Observation and the Collection and Interpretation of Data," *American Journal of Sociology,* 60 (January 1955), 354–60.

Wilson, J. A. R. "Sometimes Teachers Should Spank Children," *Educational Forum,* 24 (January 1960), 217–19.

Newspaper Articles:

"Abolishing the Cane; Danish Plans," *London Times Educational Supplement,* 2637, December 3, 1965, p. 1206.

Brockett, Tom. "Cane 'Brutal' Readers Say." *The Waikato Times* (New Zealand). August 8, 1965.

"Call for Abolition of Caning," *The Christchurch Press.* April 23, 1969.

"Cane Returns to Cardiff," *London Times Educational Supplement,* 2755, March 8, 1968, p. 782.

"Discipline in the Schools a Live Issue," *Christian Science Monitor,* January 26, 1968, p. 1.

Dunmore, Harold. "Is it the Rod that Spoils the Child?" *Auckland Star,* November 24, 1965.

Fowler, Judy. "Demands for a Return to Spanking in Schools Stir Heated Disputes," *Wall Street Journal.* June 16, 1970, p. 1.

"Hands Beaten Into Blood Blisters at City School," Letter to the Editor from Mrs. Julia White. *The Waikato Times.* (New Zealand). August 19, 1965.

Mayston, Bill. "The Case For and Against the Cane," *The Christchurch Star.* June 17, 1969.

"Minister is Thankful for Hidings," *Wellington Evening Post.* April 19, 1965.

"Petition Seeks Ban on Corporal Punishment," *The Christchurch Press,* May 29, 1969.

"Scottish Faith in the Power of the Rod," *London Times Educational Supplement,* 2658, April 29, 1966, p. 1307.

"Taws, Strap and Belt: Maintaining Discipline North of the Border," *London Times Educational Supplement,* 2594. February 5, 1965, p. 346.

"Trade Issue Stirs New Zealanders," *New York Times,* May 16, 1971, p. 9 (Special to the New York Times from Auckland, New Zealand, May 15, 1971).

Yeo, Bruce and Connie Schreiber, "Discipline Compromise Draws Criticism," *Syracuse-Herald Journal,* August 26, 1968, p. 21.

Other:

Bourne, Harold. "The Family," a talk given by the author, a Lecturer in Psychiatry at the University of Otago Medical School, 1958.